I DID NOT KILL MY HUSBAND : BUT I ALMOST KILLED MYSELF

A CANDID MEMOIR: THE HARD TRUTHS OF HEALING TRAUMA CAUSED BY THE DISEASE OF ALCOHOLISM

AM PARKER

CONTENTS

FOREWORD

Annie is both a teacher and a storyteller... Of truth. Truth she's found in life experiences that forced her to lean into the pain and rise from the death grip of trauma and tragedy. This book is her story of how she has transmuted and pushed forward to heal from the emotional darkness.

I've known Annie from adolescence to marriage to kids to divorce. Together, we have danced seasonally to the same common miserable tunes that life can upheave. Misery... It can come in droves and then subside.

Wash, rinse, repeat.

As you walk alongside your bestest friends, through life's fires together, you begin to fully understand the depth of their pain. Walking through fires together allows us to support one another's pain when it becomes too heavy to carry alone.

Sometimes one of us holds the water bucket while the other feels like they're burning. We take turns through the seasons of life. And yet other times, we can walk out of the flames both carrying water to help put out other fires.

Even though Annie and I have spent many years side by side, I am no stranger to witnessing the devastation and destruction alcoholism can have on an afflicted one. And, residually, the loved ones surrounding them. I, too, know the powerlessness you can feel and the silence and secrecy this disease hides in.

Annie is here to break the chain and give you resonation, insight, and encouragement that there can be clarity out of the chaos; there is light to be found. She'll take you into the darkness that lies deep within, and hand you a light so you can see more clearly.

Whether you're in the trenches and feeling the fire of having an alcoholic in your life, or just looking for resonation, this book takes a deep dive into Annie's life experiences, the trauma of alcoholism, surviving and thriving, and ultimate healing. She has a gift to be able to turn her mess into a message. I trust her ability to be so vulnerable in telling her own story that it will give you strength to keep going. She'll reassure you that you, too, can find your way out.

Keep showing up. You're not alone.

Casey.

For E, E and W:

All of the ugliest parts of life have given us the most beautiful existence together.

Life is short but sweet for certain.

"Thank you so much for all you do for me and the boys. I love you very much. You are amazing. You are a wonderful wife and person. I would be lost without you."

"I miss you guys! I hope you're being good for Mommy! Daddy is busting his butt off here and will be home before you know it! I will make sure to try and contact you guys as much as possible. Please take care of Skeeter for me. He will need a sleeping buddy at night. Also take good care of Mommy. Give her lots of hugs and kisses. I will miss all of you VERY much. I love all of you very much and you will see me before you know it! And when I get back, lots of games and whatever you want to do!"

Chris, to his wife and sons upon entering rehab, eight months before he died.

A LETTER TO MY READERS

Welcome. This is a safe place and I'm so glad you've found your way here. Based on the title of my story and the fact that you're choosing to read it, I have to believe that you, too, have loved someone who was sick with the disease of alcoholism.

I'm well aware that anyone who chose this book was not looking for light bedtime reading, but is here in pain and with purpose and conviction.

The events in my memoir are true and are very personal to myself and my family. After my husband died, I promised his soul that I would tell our story in an attempt to help as many people as possible. I promised myself that I'd make sure Chris didn't die in vain. This is me keeping true to my promises.

Not only do I hope to help families as they battle this devastating disease, I specifically want to focus my efforts on the spouses of alcoholics. We, too, suffer greatly through this disease and sit in silence.

Before we do anything powerful and life changing, it's important to know our why. My why is simple. Alcoholism is a very silent, secretive killer. So many families are suffering from this disease, and keeping it secret - just like we did.

This disease killed my husband, my children's father, and it almost killed me - and I wasn't even the drinker. It can feel really unsafe to talk about alcoholism and being married to an alcoholic out loud. Why? Because of the giant stigma surrounding it. Well, it's about time for this villain to get outed. I'm here screaming, doing my part to put an end to that stigma.

I'm writing this for those who, for a thousand different reasons, have found it difficult to find peace in their lives, and who have been pushed by unfair circumstances to the darkest and most painful of places.

I'm writing to those who have been left feeling broken by the cruelty of all the losses they've accumulated in the wake of this disease; devastating subtractions like people who have died, left you voluntarily, or whom you've been forced to push away in order to protect yourself.

I'm writing to those who have watched the dreams you've dreamed dissolve into thin air - despite how much of yourself you sacrificed while trying to make all the things come true that should be true, but are not.

You most likely chose this book with weary hands, mustering up enough strength to search for any light at the end of a very long and dark tunnel. I want to help ignite the spark to that light you're searching for so desperately.

Nothing I say in this memoir will fix or change your loved one's situation; that's an impossible task. But, if you're seeking guidance while navigating the devastation of someone else's alcoholism, you're in the right place. I'm here to help.

I wrote this memoir for you, as an ally, knowing how much I needed it a decade ago when I was on the front lines myself. Alcoholism is a very isolating and misunderstood disease, preying upon everyone in the alcoholic's inner circle.

I hope that reading my story helps build your courage and understanding so you can find your own path to healing. Though I don't have all the right answers, I do; however, have experience, strength, and hope for you.

God, I'm going in. Cover me...

Annie

I

MY AGONIZING AWAKENING

"Family dysfunction rolls down from generation to generation, like a fire in the woods, taking down everything in its path until one person in one generation has the courage to turn and face the flames. That person brings peace to their ancestors and spares the children that follow."

— TERRY REAL

Not too long ago, I found myself standing a foot away from the tracks of an oncoming freight train, seriously contemplating taking just one step forward and ending my own life.

A single step forward is all it would have taken to not just end my life, but more importantly... End my suffering.

One tempting step was all that stood between me and the promise of relief from all the excruciating pain that was suffocating me.

Obviously, I chose not to end my life that day. I used to secretly think to myself that stepping away from that train was the hardest thing I ever had to do. Well, it wasn't, because burying my husband was.

Shortly after I decided not to kill myself, my husband was found dead on the floor of his childhood bedroom. He was naked, in the fetal position, stone cold, and all alone, with only his beloved dachshund by his side.

The culprit? The disease of alcoholism. I think. Or, was it me? Sometimes the line feels a little blurry.

Can we take a moment and just breathe together here?

I have something I need to be up front with you about from the start. You see, if I'm being completely honest, the title of my memoir may be a tad iffy. Some days I'm not really sure if I killed my husband or not. I definitely have been accused of it by a handful of people.

I even told my husband I was going to kill him once in a fit of rage, hyperbolically of course. On top of that, I often wished him out of my life while we were married. It goes without saying, I did a lot of things wrong in our marriage and I carry a lot of guilt around with me.

The broken parts of me, the parts of me I'm still frivolously trying to heal, from the aftermath of living with an active alcoholic for a decade, often make me question it all.

Look friend, if there's one thing I know for sure, it's that I cannot be the only wife, girlfriend, mother, daughter, or friend of an alcoholic who has struggled silently with suicidal thoughts; thoughts provoked by feeling completely overwhelmed and just plain stuck.

If you, too, are struggling with the daunting task called picking up all the shattered pieces of the things everyone else is flippantly breaking in your life, you're in the right place.

Oh, it's not your spouse who's battling a drinking problem? That's okay, you're still in the right place. You can replace the word spouse with any fitting noun: parent, child, friend, loved one…and any of these will work.

I hate to be the bearer of bad news, but alcoholism is a family disease. That means your entire family is suffering from your loved one's drinking.

Though extremely scary and uncomfortable, it's important to me to tell my story and reach anyone who might benefit or find comfort in hearing my experience of being married to an alcoholic for ten long and eventful years.

I've decided that if I'm going to do this, I'm cracking myself wide open and doing it in its entirety - no matter how unpleasant it feels.

Being vulnerable, completely exposed, and daring to be seen from the inside out is... Like really freaking hard you guys. It literally feels like I'm sitting in front of you naked, legs spread on exhibit.

Well, here I am in all my glory.

I am shouting at the top of my lungs to anyone here who's reading this because they, too, feel submerged beneath the ruthless and unforgiving heaviness of an arduous life.

I'm crossing my fingers that anyone who reads my story understands that... It's *my* story; written accounts of my actual life experiences.

I'm a mom and a small-town teacher. There are a lot of little ones looking up to me as a major role model in their lives, as well as grown up adults whom I taught all the way back when I started teaching 17 years ago. I still see my past students around town frequently.

Teachers are supposed to be these flawless, perfect people who don't have real feelings, make mistakes, experience hard things, or even cuss. But that's not reality; teachers are humans just like everyone else.

But, what that means is that there's been an added level of hesitation for me to write my story and publish it for all to see. It isn't easy to say faux pas type things out loud like... I almost killed myself... When I know more than just my target audience is going to read it.

Look, I've thought really long and hard about writing this memoir. It isn't something I whipped up overnight with no effs given. I've come to the conclusion that I also think that being genuine about all the things I've felt and stood bravely up against in my life can be something else for young people to look up to.

Suicidal thoughts aren't something people always speak openly about, but it's a common enough issue that I feel confident in saying this: At some point, some of my students will have, or already have had, suicidal thoughts themselves. Maybe my story can help them work through their own struggles, even if they're not dealing with active alcoholism in their own lives.

1

SUICIDE

According to the CDC, suicide is the third leading cause of death among people aged 10 - 14, the second leading cause of death among people aged 15 - 34, and the fourth leading cause of death among people aged 35 - 44 years old.

Among students in grades 9 - 12 in the United States in 2013:

- 17% of students seriously considered committing suicide in the previous 12 months
- 13.6% of students reported making a plan about their method of committing suicide in the previous 12 months
- 8% of students attempted to commit suicide at least once in the previous 12 months

Among adults 18 years of age and older in the United States in 2013:

- 9.3 million adults, which was 3.9% of the adult population, reported having suicidal thoughts in the previous 12 months
- 2.7 million adults, which was 1.1% of the adult population, reported making a plan about their method of committing suicide in the previous 12 months
- 1.3 million adults, which was 0.6% of the adult population, attempted to commit suicide at least once in the previous 12 months

Center for Disease Control

I can't promise that everyone reading my memoir will like what I have to say. In fact, I know some people will be in a complete upheaval for the revelations about to occur.

I can, however, promise that everything I bring to light is the truth - *my* truth - the hard truth of the devastation of this disease. Through my experiences, I hope you find your own strength, vindication, and whatever else it is you're seeking by being here.

I have to trust myself in releasing my deepest, darkest moments, knowing my single purpose for writing it - to help others. I also know that there are two main reasons why someone has picked this book up to read.

The first, those whom I'm writing this story for, being spouses and family members of people suffering from the disease of alcoholism. People who, like the old me, are feeling lost and distraught and are looking for guidance as they journey through the trauma this disease brings into every home it enters.

And, the second, being people who either know me or my husband and want to know details of my life or of his sudden and tragic death. Either way, I welcome you all here and appreciate you taking the time to care.

From here on out, I'll be writing directly to my fellow 'loved ones of alcoholics' with complete authenticity so that I can do what I came here to do and try to help.

I'm well aware that, in your own way, you've ventured out of your comfort zone just by picking up this book and sort-of admitting you've found yourself under water.

That simple act, in itself, is not an easy thing to do. I commend you for doing it anyway and I want you to know that you're not alone. Your life doesn't have to be this way.

Read that again and sit with it for a moment. You're not alone. Your life doesn't have to be this way.

Maybe you haven't yet found yourself standing next to a freight train, summoning up every ounce of strength you have to not step in front of it. Or maybe you have. Maybe you've brought a sharp knife with you to the bathtub 'just in case' (I've done that too). Maybe you haven't.

Regardless, I'm willing to go way out on a line here and bet that if you have a spouse or family member that is an alcoholic, you've thought about ending your misery one way or another.

2

HARD TRUTH

NOT ALL OF YOUR PAIN AND MISERY IS CAUSED BY OTHERS.

A s it will be with your own journey toward healing and recovery, it's important to look back on exactly what had me standing so close to that oncoming train in the first place.

I was being dragged down by the weight of trying to break generational curses and cycles of severe, debilitating anxiety and addiction.

Then, there was that thing always lurking around called the excruciating failure of not knowing how to love myself unconditionally - especially when nobody else was.

Here's the first uncomfortable truth revealed in all of this: Not all of my misery was caused by other people, and not all of yours is either.

We could go around and around all day discussing the behind the scenes reasons why people like us struggle to love ourselves. But, at some point, we have to start accepting life on life's terms and own our part in it.

As a promise to my deceased husband, and in an attempt to help as many people as I can, I speak publicly about his passing when I have the opportunity to do so.

The first time I got to do this was powerful for me, as I found myself not only telling his story, but telling mine as well. We obviously had two very different perspectives on what happened to us.

This experience helped me to realize how the roots of my childhood played a part in getting me there. I was speaking on anger that particular evening:

> *"My journey with alcoholism started about fifteen years prior to [my husband's death] with my sister who is also an alcoholic. Interestingly enough, all of the issues and problems that [my family of origin and I] had in the past because of alcoholism came around tenfold with my husband's personal struggle with it. For me, anger is not just one thing. Anger is grief and all the emotions that come with it. It's feeling helpless and sad and worried and anxious and scared and all of those things that don't feel very good when you are living a life that is completely out of control.*

As I get to know this disease a little bit more, I realize that [my struggles] didn't really stem from my husband and his alcoholism; they started during my adolescence. Look, I can't say I had a rough childhood. I had hard working parents who always wanted what was best for their family. It's just that... what they wanted and what sometimes happened didn't always match up.

I'm not an adult who had an abusive childhood and I didn't grow up in misery. My parents aren't 'bad' people like one might expect with the challenges I've faced as an adult. They are, however, unhealthy in their own ways and have some pretty dysfunctional tendencies that are now coming to light as I am becoming healthier and more evolved myself.

My mom has extreme anxiety (due to genetics, but was definitely heightened by my sister's drug addiction and alcoholism), and my dad is filled with anger because of his own traumatic and abusive childhood. They fought often during my younger years and my sister and I were surrounded by a lot of explosive resentment.

In my unprofessional, but self-labeled expert opinion, the issue was, is, and will continue to be that my parents are not getting specified help for any of their hardships in life. So, they can't always make the healthiest decisions in their own lives.

I grew up in a home where I was loved, but I did not feel like I was loved unconditionally. I think of it as being loved 'if'. I was loved if I behaved, if I did (or didn't do) certain things, or if I listened to [my parents] and did what they thought was right. I was not allowed to have an unpopular opinion or make decisions for myself without being made to feel less than. Mistakes were punished and not looked at as something I could grow from.

I still struggle to make decisions for myself to this day. What happens when you're a child and you're treated in a way where you don't feel like your ideas and choices are good enough is... You grow up not knowing how to make decisions or mistakes without feeling really shameful.

That is the battle that I'm fighting right now. Not really knowing how to trust myself to make good decisions, I got married at the age of 23 to a man with narcissistic and abusive tendencies, who was a habitual marijuana user. Though not professionally diagnosed with narcissism, I'm just calling him how I see him. I ignored all the red flags that were there during our engagement. Then, we divorced and I married someone else who needed fixing. My second husband was an alcoholic.

I try to keep in mind that my parents too, were just doing the best they could with what they had. They

*were miserable themselves during my childhood, and
were just trying to keep it all together. I get that, I've
been there too. It puts things into perspective for me
and it keeps my own anger and resentment in check.
I wasn't always the easiest child - I went through a
huge rebellious phase during my teen years that could
send any parent through the roof. I can take
responsibility for my actions, knowing that I played
my own part in it.*

*I can't go through life every day pointing fingers,
upset with my parents, my ex, or my husband
because then I wouldn't be living a very joyful and
serene life. I'm a firm believer that as I heal, the
entire world heals along with me, in small ways,
through a ripple effect. My new and improved ideas,
decisions, and actions bring similar positivity to
those around me. And to those around them, and
so on.*

*Honestly, I'm really grateful for the hardships that
I've been through, and whatever it was that got me to
those hardships, because I'm here now living my best
life.*

*There has been lots and lots of grief and lots and lots
of anger in my life. Alcoholism is a family disease and
I'm already noticing the effects it has had on my own
young children. My youngest son portrays his anger
as extreme anxiety and fear of abandonment, and my*

oldest is the very stereotypical 'why did he love alcohol more than us' kind of angry.

So, I'm here to not only better my life, but better theirs as well. This past few years has been really, really tough."

That, in a nutshell, is an overview of the dysfunctionality I grew up with and the trauma I experienced as a young adult.

I'm not here to blame my parents or my first husband for my misery or for the decisions I made in my past. Taking their moral inventory is not on my agenda, I'm merely acknowledging that a lack of confidence in decision making and an absent sense of self worth started well before I found myself married to an alcoholic.

Whatever the reasons are that got me here, and whatever got you here too, I know this for sure - trying to learn how to love yourself as an adult is as easy as riding a bike. Uphill. Barefoot. In the dead of summer. With two flat tires.

But at the end of the day, we have to take some responsibility for our own actions and decisions. Projecting our struggles onto others doesn't allow for any enlightenment or healing.

The Good news? Taking responsibility starts right here, right now with simple cognizance. Healing here we come!

3

HARD TRUTH

TRYING TO CONTROL SOMEONE ELSE'S ACTIONS CAUSES MORE HARM THAN GOOD.

I was so close to that train that the fierce wind blew my hair back parallel to the ground, forcing my eyes shut and sending its very breath into my lungs. It threatened to shove my entire being backward as if to tell me that it didn't want me invading its sacred space.

I don't know how long I stood there before the steam from the train's mighty engine hissed to wake me from my trance. It was screaming at me, begging me to step back.

Thoughts of suicide? Me?

The successful, well-loved, beloved small-town teacher? The loving and organized 'has it all together' mother? The doting wife who always kept her husbands' secrets in order to protect them? The outgoing one who makes friends out of strangers, appreciating what each soul brings to life's table? The healthy one who exercises daily, meal preps on Sundays, and writes books and patient advocate articles for the sole purpose of helping others wade through their own struggles in life?

Yes, me.

One of my old character flaws was a need for control. You see, when everything surrounding me felt out of control, the only thing I could think to do was try and command its obedience in any way I could. Tried as I might, it never worked.

I thought maybe, just maybe, if I tried hard enough, did more, knew more, worked harder, prayed on it, and even attempted to predict the future, I could control the chaos and prevent all the bad things from happening.

I wish it was that easy, but sadly there is no magic wand in life. There's no quick fix to problems, and we don't get three genie wishes. Trying to control what others do and think is a complete waste of time and energy.

After a lot of effort toward my own healing, I've learned this very important idea: When I try to control everything around me, my life becomes unmanageable.

It's important to note here that not trying to control and relinquishing power are two very different things. Power doesn't come from controlling everything around us; it comes from the decisions we make, for ourselves, in spite of what others choose to do. That's where our power lies.

As I was standing there, I could feel the train roaring deep into every broken crack in my soul. Every single one of my bones was rumbling along with the sound of the wheels rhythmically beating the metal of the tracks. Ba-da, ba-da, ba-da... It felt good, comforting even.

Eyes closed, I began daydreaming, remembering fond times I spent in my happy place, concerts, where the sounds coming from the stage shook my bones in much the same way. It took everything in me to keep my feet planted firmly on the ground and stay put, arms by my side.

I'm a whimsical dreamer, not a lost soul. I carry around healing stones in my bra and get my tarot read twice a year for goodness sake. I'm always seeking signs, Godwinks as I call them, that I'm on my right path.

I believe in the good of others and feel connected to the universe with every fiber of my being.

I've always cared for others with my whole entire heart, but in the past could not, for the life of me, figure out how to effing love myself. I'm the one you'd never, ever, guess would be hurting enough to fantasize about taking their own life.

Is any of this ringing a bell, dear friend reading this book? We may not know each other personally, but if you have a loved one who is an alcoholic, we definitely understand each other's pain.

Specifically, what had me standing next to that train that day was the dreaded onset of my second, not first, but second divorce (aka dysfunctional relationship) before I even turned 40.

4

MY FIRST MARRIAGE

My husband, Chris, was violently losing his battle with alcohol addiction. I had an ex husband, Samael (Sam for short) - as I'll call him as an undeserving kindness, who ~~was~~, scratch that, *is* what I can only label as an emotionally abusive, narcissist.

In fact, this 'gem' even blamed me publicly for Chris's death in a disgusting cry for attention. No worries, if you're here, you get free tickets for a front row seat to all my drama. Grab your popcorn!

"Apparently, at some point, Chris began to feel the strain of the tightly controlled prison he'd conformed to for so long and began to drink. [Annie], of course, needed control over that too, so he started drinking in private, hiding it. This behavior continued, unfortunately, leaving poor Chris to look like the bad guy (he was not) and [Annie] kicked him out when he needed her help the most. As terrible as it is, [Chris] passed away from the damage done to his body from this behavior."

— MY EX HUSBAND

Ahem… You guys, *insert sarcasm and dramatic eye roll here* I am just so glad that my ex husband shared his wisdom about alcoholism with the world. I guess I should have consulted him before taking the time to write this memoir because apparently the answer is a lot less complicated than I realized: Don't be 'controlling' and your husband won't die of alcoholism. Boom, problem solved! We can all just put this book down now and resume our normal daily activities. I'm so sorry for taking up your time.

Sigh, to this day, even after more than twelve years separates us from the finalization of our divorce, Sam continues to make it his life's goal to ensure that I struggle whenever he has any say in the matter. Fortunately for me, Sam's shenanigans no longer affect me in the way they used to.

Eventual self-worth for the win!

Needless to say, marrying Chris was easy. He was kind, fun, and loving. He worked hard and helped me with my then two year old son. He actually did more than help, he was my son's dad for all intents and purposes, raising him as his own from the first time they met. Basically, Chris was everything my first husband wasn't.

I was shocked that Chris would willingly and happily offer to do things to help me. Like suggesting he stay home from work when my toddler was sick so I could go to work. I never had that kind of support before from Sam, even though he was my oldest son's biological father.

In fact, Sam would just go missing a lot when our son was young, both when we were married and when we weren't. When we were married and he was actually home, he wasn't very responsible. Which is why, when I'd become upset at his lack of care and effort with our family life, he'd call me controlling and then storm out and go MIA for however long he wanted. Things have always been extremely tumultuous with Sam to put it lightly.

As I write my memoir, I'm finding that random memories I haven't thought about in what seems like forever are popping up out of nowhere. I've decided that including some of them will add some flair and authenticity, giving you a bigger view of my struggles and insecurities.

It makes me wish I was sitting across from you at a table having coffee and snacks, sharing our stories together. In so many ways I feel connected to you, like I know you personally because of the pain and similar experiences I'm certain we share.

I distinctly remember trying to wake Sam one morning so I could leave for work. This was while we were still married and we had an infant at the time. Though my mom watched our little one for us while Sam and I worked, Sam happened to have the day off that day. I assumed he'd... Like... Get up and parent. I was very wrong.

Long story short, Sam was not happy that I 'expected' him to function... Oops, my bad for being so controlling. His exact sarcastic, snarly words to me were, "Fine, let your mom sleep in then, I'll get up and take care of the baby."

True story. What I later realized was that he wanted to go visit his girlfriend that day and the baby was cramping his fake bachelor style.

I'll give you a moment to blink and pick your jaw up off the floor at that ridiculousness.

Something my ex husband still throws in my face when he's mad at me is how controlling he thinks I am. He blames the demise of our marriage and his under par relationship with our son on my 'controlling ways'. Neither could be farther from the truth, but there's no telling Sam that.

I mention this now because I have a feeling that you, too, may understand the impulse to manage your environment when everything around you feels chaotic. It's a coping mechanism for survival.

I don't know who needs to hear this, but here's a little public service announcement: Wanting your significant other to do things like work, help clean the house, help take care of the kids, and respect you by not cheating on you... Or lying to you... Or drinking too much booze... Or smoking too much marijuana... Isn't you being controlling.

Listen Sam (and all the other shamers and blamers in our lives), nobody wants the burden of trying to keep everysinglethingintheworld together; it's absolutely exhausting. We just want to feel safe and live a life that allows for peace and happiness.

Let me be crystal clear about this, readers: If Sam (and your difficult person/people) behaved better, we wouldn't feel distressed enough to try to force changes. End of story.

Honestly, this is all part of why I struggle to know the difference between when I'm trying to control too much and when I'm simply feeling uncomfortable and needing to change my own circumstances.

To combat my feelings and a tendency to desire control over anything that has gone awry, I often spend my time researching and learning details about things to satisfy my need to understand them.

Knowledge is a little superpower of mine. Here's a field trip to the inside of my brain after a quick Google search about the train I found myself next to...

Freight trains are super heavy and super fast. They can weigh anywhere between 4,000 and 20,000 tons. Through towns, they slow down, but generally travel at speeds of 125 - 150 miles per hour. They do have emergency brake systems, but even under full use of these systems, it can take larger, heavier trains up to a mile to make it to a full stop. (railroads.dot.gov)

I have no idea how large this particular train was or how fast it was going. But I'm sure you can imagine the absolute power of any train rushing past a person that was standing only a foot away from it.

I mean, if I would have merely stuck my arm out, this massive machine would have taken my entire body with it in a flash. I didn't even really need to step forward.

Honestly nowadays, the healed parts of me that were once broken, feel disappointed in myself for getting that close to the train in the first place. You know, now that I've found my self worth, I can look back at it and realize just how stupid it was.

In the moment, however, I wasn't thinking clearly. I couldn't; I wasn't yet capable. I hated my life and I hated myself for not being able to get my shit together. I wanted my pain to stop, and that's all I could see at the time.

One of the biggest mountains I've had (to try) to climb in life has been other people making decisions for me - without my permission. How many times has that happened to you while dealing with an alcoholic or anyone else causing trauma in your life? No wonder we feel out of control; how could we not?

I mean, what if we don't *want* to live a life in turmoil and despair because of someone else's drinking or cheating or inability to be responsible or - fill in the blank with any other damaging experience? Are we supposed to just sit there, do nothing, and allow it for ourselves? I think not. It's a firm no from me.

5

HARD TRUTH

YOU, TOO, ARE SICK FROM ALCOHOLISM.

I n fact, so many others find that their attempts at controlling their surroundings causes their lives to become unmanageable that Al-Anon Family Groups, twelve-step communities that provide help for families and friends of alcoholics, as well as Alcoholics Anonymous - commonly known as AA, both state this as their first step in the recovery process:

> *"We admitted we were powerless over alcohol-that our lives had become unmanageable."*

> — AL-ANON FAMILY GROUPS

It's time to pause from telling my story for a brief moment to explain something that may be crossing your mind. You might be thinking heyyyy, is this chick really here trying to talk about a twelve-step program *for me?* Why? I'm not the one with the problem.

First, I'm not here to persuade you to do or not do anything. Attending Al-Anon meetings is a decision I made as a part of my personal healing journey, just as asking my husband to leave our family home was. What's right for me may or may not be right for you.

Second, as I mentioned earlier, alcoholism is a family disease. So... Yeah, you too are sick from this disease in a lot of ways. You aren't 'the problem', but you certainly have a problem (or a thousand and one).

Practicing the principles of Al-Anon has been imperative in my unique-to-me recovery process, so naturally I'll be mentioning it from time to time in my memoir.

Just as an FYI, Al-Anon is an option for those of us that are looking for that type of support and assistance. It is a safe place where people like us can go to share their experience, strength, and hope when combating the disease of alcoholism. It's a place to learn about it and talk with others who understand because they, too, are suffering.

This has been a major part of my passage from sick and miserable to healthy and happy - and you get to decide if it ends up being a part of yours. The beauty in all of this is that we each get to make our own decisions based on our individual experiences and needs.

Once I realized how sick I was myself, I sought help. I simply refuse to let this disease harm me or my family any longer and I needed assistance in working through it so I could make it stop.

If I'm being one hundred and ten percent honest, I don't know how I'd be standing upright today without Al-Anon. Regardless, it isn't my goal or my responsibility to give advice or promote the program. I'm simply here to carry *my* message to each of you.

If it sounds like something that would benefit you too, then I urge you to try it. If not, you do you. I love you just the same and I know you'll find your way to serenity one way or another.

II

ANNIE

"Is she dead? Is she fine? Every day, every night...

Fate has dealt me a lonely blow. Tried to help, only hurt. In the end I made it worse."

— THE LUMINEERS, LEADER OF THE
LANDSLIDE

I have a secret to tell you, I'm not actually a human. I'm a robot. A very skilled, very convincing robot. And an actress when I need to be. Don't get me wrong, I'm a truth teller and rule follower. It's just that I am also scarily capable of motioning through all of my hard days with a false smile on my face and pep in my step, pushing down all of my real feelings. Easy peasy.

I wasn't always this way, but over time I've learned how to robot as a coping mechanism for survival. Funny enough, every time I log into anything on the internet that asks me to check the box proving that 'I'm not a robot', I chuckle to myself.

6

INFIDELITY AND EMOTIONAL ABUSE

To give you a snapshot of why I found myself standing next to that oncoming train, I need to go way back to when I was married to my first husband, Samael.

I was much younger and much more naive back then and allowed him to mess with my psyche. Besides his less than stellar ability to parent and have responsibilities, I was dealing with the very deep and very painful grief that accompanies infidelity. He was cheating on me with someone at work and let's just say I didn't handle it well. At all.

Not only was Sam cheating on me, he was blaming *me* for *his* love affair. You know, because nothing is, was, or ever will be the narcissist's fault.

Clearly, if I would have been prettier, skinnier, more fun, and less preoccupied (with our new six month old baby) it would have been much easier for him to keep it in his pants. Barf.

Plus, silly me, if I had attended to every one of Sam's outlandish sexual desires, he wouldn't have 'felt the need' to cheat on me. Duh. But, like… No, I definitely don't want to ask my friend to have a threesome with us.

Yes, you read that correctly, your eyes aren't playing tricks on you. You know, come to think of it, I really should have been a better wife to Sam. Unquestionably, if I was, he would have treated me better. Maybe if I was more perfect, he wouldn't have felt the need to project his own brokenness onto me. Sure, we'll go with that.

Is anyone else chuckling along with me right now? It's probably time to profess that I plan to use a bit of sarcasm and humor throughout my story. In no way am I trying to make light of the difficult things we go through in life. I know there's a fine line between humor and being inappropriate and I promise to try to dance on the humorous side of that line.

When I was neck deep in my angst of being cheated on, I probably wouldn't have been able to find any humor in it. I very much want to respect everyone's feelings and individual stories while I write mine. But in order to make it through this whole, Imma need to mix in some funnies or else I'll just bawl the entire time I write it.

Being in my early twenties, I didn't yet know what a narcissist was. I thought it was just a demeaning term used when name-calling someone deemed overconfident and selfish.

I wasn't entirely wrong, but narcissism is much more than a rude person thinking the world revolves around them. It's a premeditated grooming of unsuspecting victims; self-centeredness on crack, if you will.

Narcissists have an incredibly terrifying sense of entitlement and an absolute lack of care and empathy for others. That's how they work. They do disgusting and awful things, then place blame and shame on everyone else, ~~even those they claim to care about most~~ especially those they claim to care about most.

I felt as small as a quark when I was married to Sam, and was absolutely confused and distraught. Quarks are broken down protons and neutrons if you're wondering. Basically, they're the smallest thing that exists.

In my younger and less evolved days, I believed Sam when he told me I wasn't good enough and that it was my fault he felt the need to stray from our marriage. His affair sucked the life out of me quite literally.

At the time of Sam's affair - with a young lady from work who donned the last name 'Generous' of all names - I was pretty distraught. See, I told you part of this is funny! She was very generous, indeed.

Trying to navigate that type of craziness was an absolute energy suck. I wasn't able to eat or sleep, and was caring for an infant all on my own while trying to work and stay afloat. It took effort just to breathe. I was 26 years old for goodness sake, and I was lost. This wasn't what was 'supposed to' happen in a marriage!

I didn't know this then, but I was being taught the hard way that... Wait for it... Life is not all sunshine and rainbows. My mental and physical health were both withering away. I went from a size 6 to a size 0 in one month's time; a decomposing zombie wandering aimlessly if you will.

The first time Sam saw me naked after he returned, he made sure to tell me how thin and sexy I looked. I was skin and bones because of how much he was hurting me; what a fucking slap in the face.

There was a new, determined, anger raging inside of me from that moment on. You better believe he never saw me naked again.

HARD TRUTH

THINGS THAT OFTEN FEEL ROTTEN ARE
SOMETIMES BLESSINGS.

W ant to know something that will blow your mind? Anger is amazing like that, friends. Its purpose is not to hurt us, but to make us feel uncomfortable enough to make a change. Anger can be a wonderful tool that helps project us toward something new and better.

Anxiety is often much the same; it says, "Hey, human! Something isn't right here. I'm gonna make you feel really awful until you make it right again."

Unevolved perspective: I hate anger and anxiety!

Evolved perspective: Thank you, anger and anxiety!

Whoa! Perspective is super important on evolutionary journeys in life. I grew up thinking anger was a bad thing when it really isn't. As a more evolved adult, I see anger as fuel, lighting a fire under my butt to go do that hard thing that seems impossible.

I like to call my journey 'From Woe is Me to Whoa! It's Me!' Wanna join me?

I try hard to use perspective in all aspects of my life now that I'm working hard at living my best life, but this is definitely something I struggled with in my past. And, how could I not struggle with it? My life was a shitshow.

My ex is the type of guy that frequently calls himself a 'grown ass man' and name calls others as an attempt to try to establish dominance. His name calling used to bother me, but now I just kind of let him say what he's going to say and then try to proceed with our conversation.

He's that douchebag you see in movies who gets off on putting other people down, and is generally unpleasant to be around. I'm speaking from my own experience here, y'all. I'm sure there are people that enjoy Sam's company.

To me, he's angry, aggressive, explosive, condescending, scary, and demeaning almost all the time. He, too, has an addiction, but of marijuana instead of alcohol and uses it as a crutch for being a bully.

Here's an example of his response to text conversation between us when I asked if he planned to pay his child support that month:

"Look [Annie], I quit smoking pot today, I'm not in the mood to put up with your shit."

— SAM

Look, I get it. I like to let loose and have a few drinks here and there. I even smoked pot a couple times in my past - trying to be a better wife and appease Sam (gross, I know - please don't judge me).

I'm also well aware that smoking pot is legal now for recreational use and that it's also used for medicinal purposes. But there is a big, humongous difference between recreational use, medicinal purposes, and dependency of marijuana.

Much like Chris couldn't make it through the day without drinking alcohol - which is also legal, Sam couldn't, and still can't, make it through his days without smoking marijuana.

My son comes home with his belongings reeking of pot after his weekends with his dad. It's pretty heartbreaking as a parent to have no control over their child being exposed to these types of things at such a young and unfit age. I rely heavily on trusting my own parenting to keep my anxieties at bay about it.

Sam's marijuana dependency and smoking habits were a huge source of tension in our marriage, and is now a huge source of tension in our co-parenting. He buys, smokes, grows, discusses, and drives under the influence of marijuana, often in the presence of our preteen son. It's inappropriate AF to say the least and, let's just say, it isn't a pastime they share passion about. It makes our son uncomfortable, as an understatement.

Divorcing Sam was the absolute best thing I could have ever done to save myself from a life of trauma. This time, my husband was in a love affair with alcohol instead of with another woman. This time, my husband was in a love affair with alcohol instead of with another woman.

I can't tell you how many times Sam got in my face during our marriage, using his voice and puffed out chest to pin me up against the wall, terrified.

He never placed a physical hand on me, but sometimes I feel like the way he treated me may have been just as abusive, if not more. At risk of being really vulnerable here, sometimes I think emotional abuse can be worse than physical. A broken bone is a lot easier to fix than a broken self worth. His demeaning ways stole the dignity right out of my soul.

Sam's method of attack is intimidation. He's always trying to deflate other people like a balloon, either by name calling or by getting loud and puffing up his chest to make himself look like a gorilla ready to fight an enemy.

Though these are just my own observations and recollections about him, remember that I'm also raising his son, and his daughter, who is not my biological child currently lives with me in my home as well.

I was definitely intimidated by Sam in my younger years. Now, I see him as a very broken, very unevolved person. However, even though I've healed from my strenuous marriage with Sam, the insecurities he meticulously instilled in me many years ago still try to slither their way back in sometimes.

That's the way this type of emotional abuse goes, and it's important for us to all understand that so it doesn't continue to cause problems in our present lives.

I actually pray for Sam's healing - for his sake and for our son's. It's best for all involved for him to heal. Plus, it has to be unbearably painful to live the way that he does. Anger hurts like a MF when you allow yourself to sit in it instead of doing something productive about it.

I have a point with all of this, I promise. While all this was going on and Sam was stomping on our marriage with his fling, I could barely make it to work, let alone do actual work. Once, I remember leaving work at lunch to go sit outside of my ex's girlfriend's apartment, waiting for him to show up so I could catch him in the act.

My boss was concerned, and made it clear that I better do something about it. That was a huge wakeup call for me. I couldn't magically fix it, but found that I was really good at pretending to be ok. So that's what I did; that's how I came to be such a proficient robot. Beep. Beep. Boop. In case you're wondering, that's 'robot' for Cheers!

That was the first really tough thing that happened to me as an adult. My first husband came back and forth as he pleased for a year or so after that, but was never trusted by me again.

He treated me like a toy that was to be played with and then tossed to the side whenever his ice cold heart desired. Remember me mentioning we had a six month old baby at home at the time?

Having a child together means I still have to deal with him frequently as our son is now thirteen, and is still a minor. One of my biggest fears is that Sam will try to turn my son into his clone with all the psychological grooming he does.

Honestly, I almost didn't even include that statement here for fear that he will read it and see it as a challenge. But, I'm here to tell my truth in its entirety. And, I have to believe in my own parenting and relationship with my son.

8

GOING BLIND

P hew! Sorry, friends, but I'm not done yet. There was so much that brought me to those train tracks. You may need a refill on that popcorn!

I had so much really hard 'stuff' going on at once that I wasn't just on the struggle bus, I was driving it. Heck, I may have even manufactured the dang thing!

Before I became an ally with the universe, I used to think the powers that be were determined to put a picture of my face in the dictionary next to the term 'Murphy's Law'. You've probably heard of Murphy's Law, it states 'What can go wrong, will go wrong.'

Now, I have my own law that I like to go by. It states, "What needs to go wrong, will go wrong" (with the purpose of keeping us all on our right paths in life, of course). We'll call it 'Annie's Law.'

For the cherry on top, as if that wasn't enough craziness already, my eyes are failing me. A decade before I found myself pondering purposeful death, at the mere age of 26, I found out I was going blind with a diagnosis of Myopic Macular Degeneration.

Deep breaths.

I already had a permanent blind spot in my central vision, black worm-like floaters constantly swimming around in my line of sight, and I was absolutely terrified of what my future was going to look like.

Myopic Macular Degeneration is exactly what it sounds like it is... A degenerative eye disease that, over time, can cause total central vision blindness. The kicker is that it's generally diagnosed as 'age-related' macular degeneration in people over the age of 65. I was 26. Cool, cool, cool...

My young and newly diagnosed self thought... Realllllly? Whyyyy me? Anything else, God? What on earth did I do to deserve all of this? What kind of unthinkable things did I do in a past life that warrants *this* of all things? Mayday!

This was my martyrdom. An unhealthy learned habit I portrayed in my past often when I played the victim role. I was young, I was grieving, and everything was exaggerated.

9

HARD TRUTH

YOU QUITE POSSIBLY... EH PROBABLY... I MEAN... ALSO HAVE MARTYR VICTIM TENDENCIES.

Y ou, too, have martyr victim tendencies. Honestly, how could you not? Life is freaking brutal. We humans simply aren't born with the right tools to know how to grieve in a healthy way. Grief, you might ask? Yep, grief.

All of these complicated emotions we experience during the hostility of the disease of alcoholism: anger, hopelessness, anxiety, depression, fear, sadness, and worry... You know, all the feels? They rear their ugly heads when we grieve the loss of the life we originally planned for ourselves.

It's time for a little disclaimer. I feel like the next few bits of my story are heavy with an explanation of my eye disease, but if you can stick with me through it, I promise I have another major point.

If I'm being totally open about it, going blind really does suck. Big time! I try to keep my game face on when I talk about it, but to put it lightly, the prospect of it is devastating.

As I stood next to the train contemplating the value of my life, I knew my vision wasn't getting any better. Ever. In fact, I could expect it to get much worse; I just wasn't sure when.

About seven years before I found myself standing in the shadows of that train, I was told that I had ten years of 'normalcy' left. That meant that by the age 36, I probably wouldn't be able to see well enough to continue living life as independently as I'd like.

I could expect to eventually not be able to see my children's faces (or their children for that matter, my future grandbabies). Everyday tasks like driving, working, and doing simple things like applying makeup and clipping toenails - anything requiring central vision precision - would slowly become tasks I could no longer do without help.

This was another personal sad truth for me. One of the hardest I'll ever face, really. Thankfully, you most likely don't have this same battle to combat along your journey. But, I know enough about life to understand that if it isn't macular degeneration you're struggling with on top of all.the.things, it's bound to be something else unique to you.

You could probably guess that a diagnosis which threatens blindness comes with a plethora of difficult emotions and, consequently, a domino effect of problems. The threat of central vision blindness was looming over me constantly.

Standing in front of that train, I only had a projected one to two more years of normalcy left with decent vision. Yet there I was, battling my husband's disease of alcoholism and a zillion other things that felt debilitatingly heavy - *instead* of dealing with my own disease and the difficult emotions that accompanied it.

You know what having a degenerative eye disease does besides steal your vision? It tries to creep in and steal your joy too. Macular Degeneration is an asshole. It makes everything else in life at least a little bit harder.

Unfortunately, pain isn't really good at compartmentalizing. And, consequently, feelings like anger and sadness become elevated when they start piling up on top of each other.

You see, when painful feelings start stacking up, we start to feel overwhelmed. Big emotions are like sparkling golden gates that open to a bridge headed toward Martyrland.

Here's the deal fellow ~~victim~~ healer, when we feel consumed by the complicated and painful 'things' in life, it becomes really easy to ask the not-so-healthy, but warranted rhetorical question, "Why me?" We've all done it and that's okay.

The reason I label this as an unhealthy question is because it has a bad habit of facilitating a mindset focused on what's going wrong rather than what we can do in order to make it right.

Martyrdom keeps us in what I like to refer to as our 'stinkin thinkin'. It can keep us stuck in a bad place if we aren't careful.

Sometimes I forget life's unwritten rules and start to feel sorry for myself when things get tough. Like, HELLO! Whoever is watching me from above, can't you see how much I'm struggling already? I don't need more really hard stuff right now. Come back another time... Or, not at all, please and thank you.

I want to be crystal clear about what I'm getting at here because so many of us are experiencing it and don't even realize it. I know that was the case for me for many years.

When we deal with so many convoluted problems at once, they eventually begin to intricately weave together. This allows the pain from each individual problem to start blending and seeping into the others; it becomes difficult to separate it all. Well, if we can't distinguish where our pain is coming from, then how can we work towards healing it?

Think of it like a braid. You start with three easy to recognize chunked out sections of hair, right? After they're criss crossed over and over again, you start to lose track of which strands are which.

The threat of blindness is braided into all of my other hardships in life. It heightens all of my emotions and often gives me a false sense of hurriedness.

In order to tackle this, I needed to find a way to separate my emotions so I could understand them and then channel them in a more positive direction. This is how I tackled the pain of my diagnosis.

When Chris was fired from his job for the second time, I realized I probably needed to get a second job to supplement his lost income. I had two little ones at home with no help and no extra time or energy to leave the house for a second shift.

I was lucky enough to land a side gig writing journal articles about macular degeneration as a patient advocate. This job fell into my lap; the company contacted me out of the blue, asking me to write for them and moderate their Website and social media page. I was nervous to step that far out of my comfort zone, but it paid well and allowed me to work from home, at my own leisure. I couldn't pass it up.

To this day, I still believe this 'job' was a gift sent from my Higher Power, to help me keep going. It was a big, huge lesson on the idea that everything always happens just as it's supposed to.

Doing this has given me more than financial freedom and the ability to keep my family in our home. It has also released me from the handcuffs chaining me to my diagnosis. Now I can focus on dealing with my other difficult things in life.

Being an advocate allows me to help others who are grappling with the physical and mental health aspects of their own eye disease.

When I was first diagnosed, it felt like a lifetime sentence of imprisonment. I felt like a young child again, terrified of a monster lurking in the closet, always ready for it to pop out at any moment to attack. Not anymore; even while my eyes noticeably continue to fail me with each year that passes by.

I had to do something positive with my diagnosis to release the death grip it had on me. I mean, a person can't exactly take a break from vision loss when they have to keep their eyes open all day every day trying to see and function.

The last thing I want to do is give my eye disease enough power over me to make my life more miserable than it needs to be. Standing next to that train, there was no way to know if I really only had two 'normal' years left with seeing eyes or not. The brevity of the possibility of it knocked me to my knees.

I no longer feel victim to macular degeneration, but empowered by it. I feel much the same with alcoholism and writing this memoir.

Alcoholism, infidelity, and macular degeneration were my joy thieves. It was emotional comorbidity at its worst; a deathly mental fuckery if you will. I stood there basking in that train's magnificence, simply not wanting to spend the rest of my seeing days in distress. I felt trapped and I desperately needed to find my worth.

Dear friends, you may want to consider investigating whatever it is that's heightening your pain and creeping in trying to steal your joy - whether it's someone else's alcoholism or a variety of complicated and painful things.

Your adventure may not include a new job like mine; just know there are so many ways to find perspective and clarity. It's important that we each figure out what works for our individual wants and needs. Sometimes that takes a little bit of trial and error.

Maybe you'll pick up a new hobby like writing or creating art or music. Maybe you'd benefit from meditation or long walks and exercise to clear your head. Maybe you'll call around to find a good-fit therapist like you've been planning to do for some time now, or even decide to check out what those Al-Anon meetings are all about.

Hey, friend, want to know something incredible? You're already well on your way to living your best life by reading this book. Curiosity is the first step in all new beginnings. You got this!

Sorting through pain and finding the source is the only way to figure out how to redirect the control it has over you. We can't always make uncomfortable feelings go away, but we can redirect them toward something more positive.

In no way, is this an easy feat, but it's imperative if you want to find your joy again. Easy isn't how we conquer our demons and grow stronger anyway. This shit takes grit.

As I write, I am in my tenth year of normalcy. In my writing, you'll find out that I'm a fighter: I don't give up easily. I started doing what I do, researching like a maniac, trying to figure out any possible way to slow the progression of my eye disease. And so far, I have!

Bear with me a few more moments here while I share a little bit of my research with you. My Mac D was a major player in what got me to that train and since this experience is slightly different than the experiences we share with alcoholism, I think this will help it make more sense.

In 2016, there was a nationwide poll conducted by the online research group, Research!America. It was found that people are more scared of going blind than they are of dying.

Adrienne Scott, lead researcher in this study and assistant professor of ophthalmology explains, "[Our] findings underscore the importance of good eyesight to most, and that having good vision is key to one's overall sense of well-being." (Research!America and Scott)

Ummm... an 'overall sense of well-being'? Ha! What's *that*? My life was f a l l i n g a p a r t! And I was going blind. Pffft... an overall sense of well being. Puh-lease.

I can joke around about my past distorted feelings now that I've done a lot of recovering from my marriage with Sam and Chris's alcoholism. But I'd like to remind you that I was standing next to a train ready to take my own life. It's needless to say that, at the time, I was desperately longing for something different, something safe in my life.

I know it may seem like happiness was just not in my cards; therefore, it may not seem like it's in your cards either because let's face it - alcoholism is also an asshole. But years later, after a lot of effort toward self evolution, I can confidently tell you this... Happiness is not only possible for you too, it's imminent if you switch your focus to yourself.

10

HARD TRUTH

LIFE DOESN'T CARE WHAT YOU'VE ALREADY BEEN THROUGH, IT WILL CONTINUE TO PUMMEL YOU RELENTLESSLY.

Look sweet friend, I know I'm shooting hard truths at you left and right and you're barely even into this book. But, I already have another hard truth for you. I know, I know... I'd like to apologize, but I really can't.

Vomiting all the hard truths at the start is just how this has to be. That's how we can get it all out in the open, and then into the thick of healing and recovery.

Sooo... sorry, not sorry?

Ummm, there's another unpleasant thing I need to divulge, and I'm just gonna get right into it. You're going to keep getting kicked while you're down.

For some cruel reason, life doesn't ever think, "Aww, she's already been through enough, I think I'll give her a break."

Life doesn't take inventory on who goes through what. It's not placing tallies next to our names every time shit hits the fan, nor is it divvying up hardships equally amongst us.

The powers that be give zero effs about it too because... Well, they know what they're doing.

You wanna know why life has to be so relentless? That's how we evolve into better versions of ourselves, that's why. We can't stop bad things from happening in life, so It's up to us to figure out how to handle whatever life decides to throw our way. One of the first things we have to do is accept that.

As I write this, I can't help but think of how often my sons whine, 'That's not fair!' I usually chuckle or grumble under my breath, then promptly retort, "Get used to it."

Life is unfair, indeed.

Something that can feel really difficult to understand when you're knee deep in anguish is that you don't deserve more pain than anyone else, and you are just as worthy as everyone else is to live an innocuous life.

The universe is simply not yet done teaching you what you need to know before your wildest dreams can finally come true. More on this later.

And, though this opinion I'm about to spew may not be popular amongst the masses, I dare say... The people who have sludged through the deepest, muddiest trenches in life (Yay you! Yay me!) are the ones that end up being stronger and more evolved in the end.

I don't mean that toward anyone in a condescending way. It's just that IMO those who have had relatively drama free lives just haven't had any practice at tackling the really gut-wrenching stuff.

I'm admittingly extremely impatient when it comes to accomplishing my hopes and dreams. Like, "Can't my dreams just come true already? I'm running out of time!" Guess what, that just isn't the way life works. I have to be very careful sometimes to not slam the gas pedal down when making decisions, but use cruise control instead. Easy does it.

As humans, we tend to measure life with time, but that's a hard pass from life; it refuses to be timed. We cannot rush our goals, ambitions, or dreams. Likewise, we cannot shoo these really hard things away or beg them to just stop.

We can't place unattainable expectations on others just because we want a, b, or c to happen bad enough. Something you need to know about expectations is that they're often accompanied by hurt feelings. Expectations really are just premeditated disappointments.

In retrospect, I can now see that I had to feel the 'go kill yourself' type of pain in order to finally make some much needed changes.

What's that? Then, how can we feel happy and at peace while life is working itself out - because you're tired of waiting and you're tired of feeling this way? I'm so glad you asked! But, uhhhh, you're probably not gonna like the answer.

Okay, here it is: We don't have control over anything in life except how we handle ourselves.

Yikes. This is a biggie!

Let's take a hot moment to let this one sink in.

All that drinking your loved one is doing? There is absolutely nothing you can do about it.

From here on out, I'll refer to 'the alcoholics' in this memoir with male pronouns. Though I've had experience with a few addicted loved ones, including my sister, the experience I had with my husband is really what disrupted my life so much that it forced drastic change.

His alcoholism is really what lit the fire in my belly to write this memoir, so he wins the pronoun game. Please, feel free to substitute my pronouns with the ones that are fitting for your life.

11

ALCOHOLISM

You may want to sit down for what comes next... The alcoholic is going to find a way to do what he wants to do. You can't pour his alcohol down the drain to stop him from drinking. He'll go get more if he wants to.

You can't restrict how much money he has or where he goes when he leaves the house. He'll find his way to the liquor store with money in hand if he wants to - even if he just got home from a 30 day stint in rehab last week.

Clearly I'm writing from personal experience here, but I venture to say you may have tried these same futile attempts to stop the drinking too. Anything to try to stop the craziness, ammiright? None of this was up to me, and none of it is up to you either. See how I gently slid that hard truth in there? I got your back.

What could you really do to stop him anyway? Quit your day job and become your own private detective? Set your entire life aside, and set up post every place he goes so you can babysit him and monitor his every move? That's not feasible.

Please don't do that to yourself, dear reader. You're not a lamb and he is not actually the devil. Stop sacrificing yourself trying to control that which cannot be controlled.

Big hugs friend, I know that's a lot to take in.

Does anyone need some more validation for my suicidal feelings (asking for a friend)? Here are some more realities of being married to an alcoholic.

Y'all, my husband lost his job twice and there were so many bills. Lawyer bills. Rehab bills. Regular bills. Unaffordable health insurance... Like, $1,700 per month unaffordable. Medical bills. Retina specialist bills. Therapy for me. Therapy for the kids. Therapy for Chris that he didn't really go to, but we paid for because - rules.

I was tirelessly working two jobs to stay afloat, in addition to the honest to goodness everyday stress of parenting and keeping up with a house - all on my own.

Chris didn't seem to care about what his alcohol based decisions were doing to me. I say he didn't 'seem' to care because I now know that he probably did actually care; he was just too sick to do anything about it.

Letting go of that control was NOT easy. Looking back on it all now, I wish I had someone with experience telling me that I had no control over any of this. It probably wouldn't have made it any easier, but I would have at least known. I thrive off of that knowledge superpower. Let go or be dragged, right?

Dramatic pause.

Friend, your life doesn't have to be unmanageable. It's important to note here that letting go of control does not necessarily mean handing over all of your power. You're not powerless when you let go of control; you always have the ability to make your own decisions and do the next best thing for yourself.

Besides all of that, I wasn't sleeping well and a lack of sleep complicates everydamnthing else in life. For me, a messed up sleep schedule is a sure sign of distress. Either I sleep too much or not enough.

When anxious, I'm either unable to sleep at night when I'm supposed to, or I fall asleep at odd times during the day. For me, daytime sleep is less like resting and more like checking out; a way to numb and not feel pain.

On my really rough nights I remember laying in bed, wide awake, visualizing myself drowning. I would be gasping for air and grasping at shadowy figures, hoping one of them would grab my flailing arms and pull me safely to the surface. Do any of you even see me struggling here????

My life was a literal nightmare.

Here's a little nugget of info for you: Proper sleep requires peace. That's probably why you're struggling to sleep properly too.

Is anyone else feeling me on any of this? That train could have stopped all of my pain once and for all. All it would have taken was one single moment of bravery and courage. A split second decision. One measly step forward... And my pain would be gone.

Snap! Just like that.

Poof... Into thin air.

End of suffering.

I'm a mom. At the time, this was the only reason why I stepped back from that train. I'd love to be able to tell you that I took a step back because I felt worthy of living life. But, I didn't find my worth until a little bit later on when I built up enough courage to ask my husband to leave our home.

Eek! I cannot believe I just wrote that out loud.

Whenever I make a decision about anything, I think about it twice; once for myself and once for my children. That sunny Sunday morning, the decision I made for my children did not match the decision I wanted to make for myself.

My unconditional love for them was shining through that morning. So I took a few steps back, even if I spent many sleepless nights after that wishing I hadn't. I may have stood there as long as I could, in awe of the train's massive presence and promised ability to end my pain, but I stepped back.

I've got stamina.

My boys needed me and I needed them. In a way, they saved my life that day. With their fathers both being how they were, I didn't have any other choice but to do whatever I needed to do to be there for them. I didn't have time to feel sorry for myself. I had to find my strength and do what women know how to do. I needed to set myself aside, literally.

I had no choice but to keep going just a little while longer, one day at a time. Sometimes, one hour or one minute at a time. Somebody had to be there for the kids' physical and emotional needs. Somebody had to work and put food on the table. Somebody needed to show the boys how to persevere.

This is what moms do. Women are warriors. We save our worries for times where we find ourselves alone after putting the kids to bed. We're professionals at holding our emotions in until we find ourselves alone in the shower or in the Target parking lot so we can have a breakdown.

I once heard the saying 'A woman's strength comes from her soul'. There isn't much more to say about that gospel except - yep.

What I didn't know at the time is that the universe has a strange way of shifting things in our lives when we're too fearful to make big changes ourselves. Everything is already planned out for us whether we like it or not. We're just here to watch it all unfold and try to find some happiness along the way.

That used to be a hard truth for me, but now I've learned to trust and find comfort in it. I'm a firm believer that the universe is always conspiring for each of us. Even through our difficult seasons in life.

In that exact moment, at those train tracks, I decided that couldn't just be that mom that said one thing and did another. I couldn't simply tell my kids that they could accomplish anything they put their minds to, but then give up on myself.

I couldn't tell these tiny humans that I was responsible for that all I wanted for them to be in life was happy... And not let them see happiness in me. I made the decision right then and there that my life was changing; our lives were changing.

Emergency brake system activated.

Full stop.

III

CHRIS

"I could have shown you all the scars at the start, but that was always the most difficult part. See, I'm in love with how your soul's a mix of chaos and art and how you never try to keep them apart.

I wrote some words and then I stared at my feet; became a coward when I needed to speak. I guess love took on a different kind of meaning for me so when I go just know it kills me to leave."

— DERMOT KENNEDY, OUTNUMBERED

Chris grew up in a small midwestern town in Southern Illinois. He was born and raised in the same house that he eventually died in 38 years later.

He grew up just down the street from his lifelong best friend and spent his childhood playing with a gang of buddies who never lost touch over the years. These young children became grown men who attended Chris's visitation with nothing but fond memories to share of their time spent together.

All but his best friend were in total shock at Chris's sudden passing, having no idea that he even struggled with alcoholism let alone that things were bad enough for him to be dead. How? Because people keep addiction secret, that's how.

In fact, Chris's best friend didn't know anything about his disease until he was all the way in a detox facility and preparing to transfer to a rehabilitation center. I reached out to him, desperate for someone who loved Chris to encourage and support him through this very difficult time in his life - someone else who wasn't me.

Though he tried, and I'll always be extremely thankful and appreciative for his perseverance, Chris all but shunned him once he knew. These are the words written by a man grieving his best friend:

> "It's taken me a week to muster up the courage to talk about my best friend Chris... We met in 1988 and we've been best friends since. Growing up, [we lived] no more than 200 feet [apart]. We played baseball in spring and summer and hockey and basketball in the fall. Summers were spent playing gutterball, snorkeling for change to get a Captain Crunch Bar, and pulling off sweet jackknives off the diving board at the city pool.
>
> 99% of my fondest childhood memories had Chris in them. I can't begin to count how many miles we put on our bikes riding to Hucks to get baseball cards or to rent Nintendo games at WW Video Store. As we grew older and went to high school, nothing really changed. We had cars instead of bikes and that was when the fun really began.

The only constant through my childhood was Chris and so on until we grew a bit older and [became] adults. Things may have changed around us, but he was still my best friend no matter what.

I remember the day he told me he was going to marry [Annie] and the day after the Cards/Cubs game that he told me he was going to be a father. I wish I could express the look of pure joy he had when he told me.

My life was so much better [because] I had Chris in it. I got to experience so much joy and frankly just fun times with [him]. I will cherish them forever. You were truly my best friend and I can't ever thank you enough for being a huge, amazing, hilarious, fun, silly, inspiring part of my life.

I love you brother, and I'll always miss the shit out of you, but I'm happy you're at peace now.

— RYAN, CHRIS'S BEST FRIEND

I've heard countless stories about the shenanigans these guys would get into as kids. Chris always spoke fondly of the fun he had with his childhood best friends at sleepovers, playing video games and street hockey, riding bikes and swimming at the community pool.

Before he had kids, Chris was happiest when he was with his friends; and he had many.

We all went to high school together; me and Chris, his closest friends, and mine. Chris and I weren't notably close in high school, but I remember him being the quiet, kind and funny kid that everyone liked.

He was a friend of friends at that point in our lives, but I remember that he was always a lot of fun to be around. Chris had a very unique and contagious laugh. It was the type of laugh that, once you heard it, you couldn't help but start laughing along with him.

Shortly after Chris passed away, this same best friend posted a video on one of my social media timelines. I remember standing in the kitchen watching it, and as soon as Chris's laugh played through my phone speakers, our youngest son came barreling out of his room, running down the hall squealing, "Is that my dad?"

Talk about heartbreaking.

Chris's laugh is certainly unforgettable. I remember laughing hysterically with him and a group of our mutual friends many times in our driver's ed class all those years ago. Even as adults, we'd sing 'Stay out of the no zone!' together whenever we'd find ourselves behind a semi truck on the highway. Chris was silly that way. That is, before he got really sick and we slowly started growing apart.

We graduated from high school together in the year 2000, then we lost touch until after my first divorce in 2010.

Chris went away to college, attending Western Illinois University, where he partied hard and was proud of it. Quiet and kind Chris from high school developed into this new, outgoing version of his more meek self... Like, becoming a DJ at a hoppin' nightclub outgoing.

Chris wasn't a big drinker in high school. In fact, he didn't drink at all back then; he was always super proud of being one of the few who didn't. But, from what I gather from his many tales of living the college life, along with the photographic evidence, he certainly made up for lost time while attending Western.

When he began drinking heavily in college, he became the life of the party, spending many of his days and evenings hanging out with friends. He thoroughly enjoyed being on his own, doing the things people do when they're away from home for the first time.

Chris was extremely intelligent, but didn't like attending the actual classes as much as he liked the idea of being away at college. He loved telling our boys the story of how amazing he was in his sleeping class; his memories of college were always fond.

Because of the love Chris had for college life, he stayed in school longer than most, obtaining his master's degree - and livin' it up as much as possible before leaving Western and heading back to our hometown.

It was then that he secured a job with some old high school friends as an IT guy, building servers at a web host company in downtown St. Louis.

Chris was also extremely proud of his memories of working downtown with his buddies. I heard many reminiscent tales of how they would often have a few drinks after work and then walk to Busch Stadium to continue the party and watch the Cardinals dominate in baseball.

To me, it seemed like Chris always longed to go back to those much simpler times, you know, before he had a family to care for; times when he didn't yet have to worry about how much he was drinking and partying.

12

CHILDHOOD TRAUMA AND
ALCOHOLISM

Alcoholism is a pathological reaction to unresolved issues and grief. Because of this, it's important to go back in time to Chris's childhood and evaluate the probable catalyst for his alcoholism.

I'd like to pause for a moment to decipher the difference between the words 'catalyst' and 'cause' here: A catalyst is defined as a person or thing that precipitates, or happens before an event, while a cause is defined as something that makes something else happen.

So, when I say things like 'the catalyst for Chris's alcoholism', I do not mean the cause of his alcoholism; I am not placing blame. Blame can't and shouldn't ever be placed on such an intricate and complicated situation.

I simply mean something that happened before his alcoholism; specifically something traumatic that carried a lot of weight throughout Chris's life.

13

HARD TRUTH

GENETICS PLAY THEIR PART IN ALCOHOLISM, BUT THOSE UNRESOLVED ISSUES NEED SOME TENDING TO.

H ey, sweet friend? Your loved one who is suffering from alcoholism most likely has unresolved issues and grief from their past as well. It's important for alcoholics (and those of us who deal with them on a frequent basis) to know this information because if left unaddressed, they will continue to be underlying issues. These underlying issues are especially talented at slowing or even preventing the addict's recovery process.

Unresolved issues are like viruses. They sneak their nasty little invisible selves in and inject their demons into each and every one of our body's cells. They can make us really sick... With the single goal of infiltrating us and taking us down completely.

Speaking of viruses, it's time for us to have a lil sidebar chatty chat. Alcoholism and heredity, come onnnn dowwwn. I said that in my best Bob Barker voice, how'd I do? Buckle up, buttercups because this is where genetics, and the good ol' nature vs. nurture debate come into play.

Look, friends, Imma be up front with you from the get go. I'm a pretty intelligent human. I can write a whole lotta words together in an order that makes sense. I mean, yeah, I can be a total ditz and hilariously clumsy sometimes, but my brain works pretty good (see what I did there?). I gotta say, while researching this topic, I realized that I'm smart, but for sure not geneticist smart.

This research, though fascinating, was intense and... Ummm... Super hard to understand at first. I promise to do the best I can to relay this information to you with a more 'regular human' type of explanation.

According to PMC US National Library of Medicine and National Institutes of Health, in an article titled 'Genetics and Alcoholism':

"There is overwhelming evidence that genetic variations contribute to the risk for alcohol dependence (alcoholism), the most severe alcohol use disorder, [and that] alcohol dependence is a complex genetic disease."

"Alcoholism has long been noted to run in families, but that alone is not sufficient to demonstrate that genetic factors contribute to risk. Many independent lines of evidence point to genetic contributions to its etiology, [or cause for the disease]."

"It should be emphasized that while genetic differences affect risk, there is no "gene for alcoholism," and both environmental and social factors weigh heavily on the outcome.

"Genetic factors affect the risk not only for alcohol dependence, but also the level of alcohol consumption and the risk for alcohol-associated diseases, including cirrhosis and upper GI cancers. Knowing that genetic factors affect risk does not mean that we know which specific variants contribute, nor how. This is an area of active research as new genes and variants are being identified."

"It is likely that, as for most complex diseases, alcohol dependence and AUDs [Alcohol Use Disorders] are due to variations in hundreds of genes, interacting with different social environments."

"[Interestingly], adoption studies show that alcoholism in adoptees correlates more strongly with their biological parents than their adoptive parents."

— EDENBERG AND FOROUD

To sum it up, both genetics and environment, including traumatic events in childhood, play their part in the onset of the disease of alcoholism. As of now, there isn't a single gene that shows up in people specifying alcoholism. There are, however, certain genes that are known to show risk of acquiring the disease; therefore, alcoholism is labeled as a genetic disease.

It's important to note that not everyone with childhood trauma turns to alcohol as their coping mechanism, and that childhood trauma doesn't have to be present in order for someone to struggle with the disease.

Sure, Chris's alcohol consumption significantly amped up when he went away to college. But this, in itself, was not reason enough for the onset or the severity of his disease. If anything, Chris's drinking days in college showed him that alcohol does a fantastic job of numbing all the intense feelings he wanted to escape.

Alcohol protects its victims from their own unwanted thoughts and feelings. And then it kills them.

Yeah, I know that last statement was quite dramatic, but it happens.

Look at it this way, in college, Chris's drinking was twofold: To have fun and to numb the pain associated with deep seated, unresolved (and probably unrecognized) issues from his past. As an adult, Chris's drinking was mostly the latter of the two. Drinking stops being fun when it starts to be a necessity.

You're probably wondering what the heck Chris experienced in his childhood deemed traumatic enough to affect his life so drastically.

Though it wasn't just one thing - is it ever - what affected Chris in such a catastrophic way all stems from one thing. And is heightened by the way in which it was handled, or the lack thereof, after the fact.

Chris's mom unfortunately passed away from cancer when he was just 5 years old. If you're a parent, or... Like, if you've ever just been around a five year old, you know just how bonded they are to their parents; especially to their mothers.

After his mom passed away, little Chris was experiencing big grief and didn't receive any type of therapy or professional help to assist in his healing and processing of such a devastating and traumatic event.

As an adult, Chris didn't talk much about his memories of his mom, but when he did, he did so with a lot of visible discomfort and sadness.

I've always believed in my heart of hearts that the loss of his mother was not only excruciatingly painful for Chris, but also more detrimental to his emotional development and well-being than anyone realized at the time.

I mean, how could it not be?

Think about it, the death of a loved one is extremely hard for any adult to process, let alone, a 5 year old baby trying to process it on his own.

HARD TRUTH

ALCOHOLICS DON'T WANT TO BE ALCOHOLICS; IT'S JUST ACTUALLY THAT HARD TO STOP DRINKING.

The inability to cope with that deep seated pain and trauma from the loss of his beloved mother in childhood is what facilitated the continuation of Chris's drinking after college. Yep… that shit snuck in with a vengeance over twenty years later.

Likewise, that deep seated pain and trauma from your loved one's childhood is also facilitating the continuation of his drinking in adulthood.

Chris and I got married and started raising a family. His life was changing rapidly and he was excited about it, but his mental health just couldn't keep up.

Abstaining from drinking, for alcoholics, is a huge mountain to climb, friends. I've yet to hear one story about an alcoholic who wanted to be an alcoholic.

Let's briefly dissect this ultimate struggle: Not only is an alcoholic's body physically addicted to it, causing an actual need for it in their systems to function (while it simultaneously kills them by shutting their body systems down), their minds simply cannot handle the stressors of life's past and present.

I believe, without a doubt, that Chris wanted to stop drinking more than anything, but his pain was just too extreme. His body and mind became too dependent, and he literally couldn't stop.

Naturally, my curiosity about this grew substantially when my own young sons lost their father at such young ages. I can't help but wonder about the lasting effects it will have on them. This is why we talk openly about their feelings and about their dad at home, as well as why they are each in intense therapy with a professional.

I need to take a moment to be unmistakably direct with you about my intentions here, dear readers. In no way whatsoever am I accusing or blaming anyone for Chris's alcoholism or his death.

I've been blamed, myself, and that shit is painful.

While evidence shows that losing his mother at such an early age, coupled with not receiving therapy to learn to cope and process such a traumatic childhood event, was the catalyst for his disease, there is absolutely no blame being placed.

Though an extremely unfortunate, tragic and trauma-filled childhood experience, Chris's mom didn't choose to be sick with cancer. And she certainly didn't choose to pass away leaving her 5 year old baby behind to grieve. Nor did his dad completely understand what to do about it; I'm sure he was doing the best he could at the time, while grieving the loss of his wife himself.

Remember how I said I like to research a lot to understand the world around me? I always had my own ideas of why Chris was in so much pain, and consequently, became an alcoholic. Well, I knew that when writing it out for my memoir, my own ideas wouldn't be enough to prove the underlying issues leading to Chris's alcoholism. So, naturally I did a lot of research on the topic.

Y'all, this is extremely important to me for two reasons. First, I have my own two children and I worry a lot about how their adult lives will be affected by their dad's alcoholism. Second, sometimes I feel like some of my decisions and actions were accomplices in Chris's death. However, just as Chris's parents are exonerated from blame, I should be too.

And, I've been bound and determined to prove to myself the validity of that so I can stop freaking obsessing over it every single day of my life. Now, I can not only boldly stand and say, I did not kill my husband, I have proof to back me up.

As a mom of young children myself, I remember thinking about how I couldn't imagine the severity of how difficult something like losing a parent would be on a child. That is, until it happened to my own.

Children that lose their parents anytime, but especially when so very young, need professional help such as psychological therapy, in order to process and heal from the trauma that type of loss brings. Their maturing brains lack the ability to process such a complicated thing on their own.

Here's what I found in my research: According to the National Institute on Alcohol Abuse and Alcoholism, in an article titled 'Childhood Trauma, Posttraumatic Stress Disorder, and Alcohol Dependence', children exposed to severe adversity early in life are at increased risk of subsequently developing mental health problems, including alcohol dependencies. Studies show that there is:

"A robust and positive relationship between exposure to early-life trauma and alcohol-related problems later in life. People with trauma-related symptoms and other negative consequences of early-life trauma may use alcohol to help mitigate such symptoms. Evidence from both animal and human research suggests that early stressors can lead to neurobiological changes in systems known to be involved in the pathophysiology of depression, anxiety, and substance use disorders, in addition to

the long-lasting effects of early trauma has specific effects on the neurotransmitter systems involved in the positive reinforcing effects of alcohol and drugs, particularly the brain pathway for dopamine."

— BRADY AND BACK, NIAAA.ORG

Specifically interesting to me in this study was the information regarding maternal separation:

"[A] series of studies... demonstrated that <u>repeated periods of maternal separation</u> in the early life of rats decreased dopamine transporter expression and increased dopamine responses to stress and behavior responses to stress, cocaine, and amphetamine. These findings suggest that early-life experiences can affect the development of the mesocorticolimbic dopamine system and <u>lead to a vulnerability to addiction later in life</u>. Thus, in addition to effects on stress reactivity, <u>early-life events might predispose individuals to the development of alcohol use disorders by directly influencing the reinforcing effects of alcohol</u>."

— BRADY AND BACK, NIAAA.ORG

Another interesting study, though extremely sad to watch, called 'Mother Love - Monkey Maternal Deprivation Experiments' shows the importance of a mother in their child's life. Warning, you'll need to grab some tissues if you decide to watch this.

Chris remembered missing his mom a lot as a young child. When he had his own little ones at home, he would often mention small things he didn't get to experience with his own mom.

Christmas Eve traditions, for example, were always something Chris didn't have memory of as a child. He was aware of things like Santa eating cookies, but he never actually left cookies out for Santa to his recollection.

Chris very outwardly hated anything Christmas: The traditions, the gifts, the music... And he struggled to get into the holiday spirit each year. He did humor me and the kids and played along, helping us put out cookies and milk for Santa as well as carrots out for the reindeer. He was a wonderful dad.

When Chris actually would talk about his mom, he'd tell stories of her being all but erased from his memories... Pictures removed from the walls and never really spoken about again at home. His dad remarried, but from what I gather, his step mom didn't treat Chris very well.

Chris is buried with his mom now.

Something surprising that I didn't know when we were married was the location of his mom's final resting place. The first time I saw it was when I was burying Chris. They're both buried less than a mile away from the first home Chris and I purchased together. I find it strange that we never visited her. I'm not even sure if Chris knew where she was buried or not.

Phew! Hey sweet friends, I have another truth to tell you that is going to be super hard to hear.

15

HARD TRUTH

ALCOHOLISM IS A LIFE SENTENCE.

W hen alcoholics are sober, they are considered in recovery only if they're attending Alcoholics Anonymous, or AA meetings. I know it may feel like I already divulged the hard truth, but I haven' t yet.

Here it is: Though they may have prolonged periods where they're able to forego drinking alcohol, alcoholics very rarely stay sober, or in recovery, if they're not working an AA program. Alcoholism is not a disease that can be cured or healed.

Doctors call this phenomenon 'dry drunk'. According to a 2010 Psychology Today article titled 'Being Sober versus Being in Recovery', "A 'dry drunk' is someone who is sober but is struggling with the emotional and psychological issues that led them to have a problem with alcohol in the first place." (Benton, Psychology Today)

There is a very big difference between not drinking and being in recovery. This is much the same for us as loved ones of the alcoholic, and why I eventually began attending Al-Anon meetings and 'working a program' myself.

We loved ones may not need to stop drinking or stay sober, but we certainly do need to recover from this catastrophic disease. It's quite a mountainous task.

To me, Chris always seemed uncomfortable in his own skin when he wasn't drinking. On top of that, he wasn't ever 'himself' after his first hospital stay, drinking or not.

But, for a while, he was at least able to refrain from drinking. He was helping at home, and trying hard to take care of himself and our family.

I didn't know the importance of alcoholics working a program at the time, nor did I know the importance of their spouses working their own Al-Anon program. So, I'm here, letting you in on the secrets I learned through my experience. Do with it as you see fit.

I've always wondered if things would have worked out differently for Chris if I would have known this back then, but I can't change the past. All I can do is let you in on my insight, in hopes that it somehow helps you along your own journey.

16

PAWS

There is another occurrence that can happen to sober alcoholics known as post-acute withdrawal syndrome (PAWS), or protracted withdrawal. This is where alcoholics who are not currently drinking experience severe mood swings, anxiety, and depression after ending their use of alcohol.

According to UCLA's Semel Institute for Neuroscience and Human Behavior, a whopping 75% of people who stop drinking alcohol experience some degree of this syndrome. (UCLA)

This would explain the drastic change in Chris's personality and behavior, even long after he stopped drinking.

When Chris was sober, he lost all sense of self. He withdrew inside himself and anyone who knew him could tell that he was battling something deep within. It was hard to watch, honestly, knowing he was struggling with so much from his past.

It's really hard to explain how long-term abuse of alcohol affects someone's brain. PAWS describes the medical reasons for the changed behavior in an alcoholic, but noticing the changes isn't as simple as the medical terminology makes it seem.

Chris stopped doing much of anything other than working, parenting, and playing XBox. He even became detached from his cherished friends. Whenever I encouraged him to reach out to them for some 'friend time', he said he didn't want to because it was hard to be around them while they were drinking.

I get that, but I also wonder if, given the chance, they could have hung out with him every now and then - sans alcohol.

If I suggested he tell them what was going on, he responded with a firm no. He was embarrassed and kept everything inside. I even tried the old 'if they're your real friends they won't judge you' talk, but he had already made up his mind, which didn't surprise me. Chris was very firm in his beliefs and wasn't easily swayed in anything in life.

It's really hard to admit that you have such a problem to others when you struggle to admit it to yourself.

The UCLA article about PAWS also explained the working parts of this phenomenon. Scientists believe that the literal physical changes to the brain that occur during the period in which the person is abusing alcohol are responsible for both the increased tolerance to the alcohol (during extended periods of drinking) and the recurring symptoms (after ceasing drinking). (UCLA)

Something that the majority of Chris's friends don't know is how sick he truly was. They only knew what Chris told them, what he wanted them to know and nothing more. Over the years, they lost touch with him, and during that time, Chris's behaviors and alcoholism started to spiral out of control.

This ultimately became a recipe for disaster. When Chris died, his friends were surprised, to say the least. Most people were because they, and I quote... "Didn't know things were *that* bad."

Sigh, I cannot even tell you how many times I heard that in the weeks succeeding Chris's death.

I so very much wish that I knew about all of this PAWS research when Chris was alive, but I just didn't. Though I'm not even sure what I would have or could have done differently if I did know about it.

More guilt.

I'd like to think that what I would have tried to do was control my reaction to the complete dysfunction surrounding me all those years. I would have made it a point to be more empathetic and kinder to Chris instead of being so angry and frustrated with him.

Like, that time I completely lost my shit when the cops rang our doorbell in the middle of the night after Chris didn't come home from 'going to an AA meeting' and went drinking instead.

You know, right after he was just hospitalized for all.the.things, was kicked out of the house, and moved back in with the promise of working a program and staying in recovery?

The neighbors noticed him driving erratically and called the police on him. When the police arrived, they could see him passed out, literally, in the middle of the living room floor, face down.

I explained to them, telling only a half truth, that he had just been released from the hospital and was adjusting to his new medication. More lies, this time by me. This was my enabling.

I asked the cops not to arrest Chris, promising to keep a closer eye on him and not allowing him to drive until things were sorted out. They agreed, but instead of feeling relief, I just felt all alone. I had no idea what to do next.

In retrospect, Chris getting arrested would probably have been better for him than to continue not having severe consequences for his very dangerous actions. I was too new to this disease to understand that at the time.

He was able to stay sober for a lengthy amount of time after this incident. Back then, I truly thought I was helping him, but I most certainly was not. You see, without consequence and without working an AA program, it's nearly impossible for a person to stay sober.

More freaking guilt.

HARD TRUTH

IF YOU CONTINUE TO ENABLE THE ADDICT, YOU'LL EVENTUALLY BURY HIM.

Well, after I learned this ultimate hard truth the hard way, I'm here to scream this as loud as I can: THESE CONSEQUENCES ARE AN INTRICATE PART OF RECOVERY FOR ADDICTS. Have you ever heard of the term 'rock bottom'? Rock bottom refers to a time or an event in the alcoholic's life where they feel things can't get any worse.

It's this feeling of 'rock bottom' that can change an alcoholic's or addict's trajectory and cause them to start making necessary changes in order to get better.

It's often said that without hitting rock bottom, addicts don't generally seek help and recovery. Each person's rock bottom is different, so it's not something we can force upon our alcoholic loved one - believe me, I tried.

Events that can get an addict to rock bottom are harsh. They're events like becoming homeless, losing custody of their children, jail or prison time, near death experiences, and loss of jobs and income.

Chris never hit rock bottom. All of those except for jail time are things that happened to him and yet, this disease still took his life. I guess death was *his* rock bottom.

Obviously, these are not easy things to watch someone you care about go through. The idea is, however, if they don't go through them… Why would they ever choose to change their behaviors? For the addict, it's called rock bottom, but I think of it as tough love.

In the addiction world, preventing these harsh consequences is called enabling.

The Betty Ford Clinic defines enabling as shielding people from experiencing the full impact and consequences of their behavior. They list these items as some specific enabling behaviors:

- Protects the addict from the natural consequences of their behavior
- Keeps secrets about the addict's behavior from others in order to keep peace
- Bails the addict out of trouble

- Attempts to control that which is not within the enabler's ability to control
- Makes threats that have no follow-through or consistency
- 'Care takes' the addicted person by doing what he/she is expected to do for him/herself

Hazelden Betty Ford

I have done them all.

I'm gonna be blunt here. It's really, REALLY hard to allow your loved one to experience consequences for their destructive behaviors.

Nobody wants someone they care about to get arrested or hospitalized, or even go through pain. Plus, it's really hard to keep our emotions in check when these things come about.

The idea of rock bottom is part of why I asked Chris to move out of our home both the first and second time around, you know, trying to force him into changing his bad habits. Haha, silly me.

To put it simply, I thought he'd miss us enough to want to change. Now that I'm more removed from the situation, I think he did miss us enough; he was just too deep into his disease to have the ability to change.

Many people don't know this, but enabling is really just a form of codependency. Codependency is defined as a focus on others' problems, feelings, and needs at the expense of your own well being. It's basically caring so much you hurt yourself.

It makes sense, right? How will an alcoholic ever hit rock bottom if someone's always there to slow their fall?

I will always have to wonder if Chris would still be alive and well today if he would have been arrested that night. Maybe, maybe not. There's no way to ever know, but it's one of those things I can't stop wondering.

IV

FLIRTING WITH DEATH

> *"The worst part about anything that's self destructive is that it's so intimate. You become so close with your addictions and illnesses that leaving them behind is like killing the part of yourself that taught you how to survive."*

— LACEY L, HEALTHYPLACE.COM

Let's go back in time to when Chris and I first became a couple. After my first husband, Sam, moved out, we divorced, and I was finally free to start living my life again. My little one spent every other weekend with Sam's mom. Sam was rarely around because - well, responsibilities are hard ya know?

It was then, on Cinco de Mayo, that a mutual friend reintroduced Chris and I to each other, ten years after we graduated high school together. We were inseparable from that moment on.

It was a whirlwind of a summer. Just three months after we reconnected, on Chris's 28th birthday, we had a shotgun wedding. A month later, I was pregnant with our youngest son, and the rest is history.

When Chris originally moved in with me and my then two year old son, we spent our evenings and weekends at home hanging out watching scary movies, horrible reality TV (Hoarders and 16 and Pregnant, anyone?), and drumroll, please... drinking vodka.

You know I feel some guilt I'm trying to heal surrounding this too.

We were just starting a new relationship, spending time together, and having fun. Looking back at it all now, I know that his drinking problem started well before we became a couple; I just had no idea. Drinking at home like we were, only enabled it.

My sister had been a drug addict and alcoholic for many years before Chris and I got together so I knew the warning signs of alcoholism.

Chris didn't act like an addict at all. He was functioning, working, helping me with my son and with keeping up the house. I think that because he helped me in ways in which Sam didn't, it was easier to look past some of the red flags at the start.

I had no idea alcoholics could function like that so it didn't even cross my mind that he may be struggling.

After we got married and I became pregnant with our youngest son, I stopped partying and drinking, annnd Chris didn't. That's when I really saw a few of those red flags, and began noticing just how much he drank on a daily basis.

By this time, we were married, owned our home together, and I was pregnant with my second child. Not that I would have left Chris right away for drinking too much, but it wasn't something I could easily find my way out of anymore if I wanted to.

Fun and outgoing Chris was the Chris I married. This Chris, I came to find out fairly quickly after we wed, was also drunk Chris.

When we were first married, Chris was an IT guy for a prestigious online brokerage firm in the city. He built servers and monitored them during third shift.

Since he worked overnights, he was alone in the building, accompanied only by the cleaning crew. One thing led to another and at some point, he was caught drinking. I never got the full or real story behind this, so this is all I know.

This was the first time (of two) that he was fired for drinking on the job. He had a very believable but entirely fabricated story about why - both times.

For this first job lost, he went into great detail about not catching a mistake with a server that caused a big enough problem for the company to fire him. No write up and no warning, blah blah blah.

Something didn't feel right about the situation, but I had no reason not to believe him - yet. This was, from what I remember, Chris's first major lie to me. They just kept coming nonstop after that.

I realized something was very wrong when I started noticing some odd behaviors at home. I began finding empty liquor bottles hidden in strange places around the house. Places like the toilet tank and the weird cabinet above the refrigerator that nobody in the history of ever actually uses.

He started carrying around a "water bottle" with him at all times. It clearly wasn't filled with water, but with his drink of choice, vodka.

From what I've been told, vodka is a fairly common drink of choice for alcoholics since it is clear in color. In my laymen expertise, I've also found that it's harder to smell on the breath than other types of alcohol. You're welcome.

Chris had also started sleeping at random, odd times of the day, and staying up all hours of the night. He got in a few car accidents and received a DUI.

His 'holly jolly' DUI happened while his sons and I waited for him to arrive at a Christmas party from work. We were gathering at my best friend's house. He called me from jail, needing me to bail him out, as I sat under the tree opening gifts with our baby on my lap.

The red flags had flown away and I was left with bright red warning lights flashing at me, screaming to me that something was not right.

He was distraught with the loss of his job and started drinking more and more. As he drank more and more, he tried to stop drinking and immediately found himself sick. He acted erratically and became violently ill when he didn't have any alcohol in his system. This ended up being a deadly game he played often. Back and forth we went, over and over again. And then over and over again some more.

18

HARD TRUTH

STOP WAITING TO SEE JUST HOW RED THE FLAGS CAN GET. RED IS RED.

I t's important to note that I didn't notice this pattern until much later in our marriage. It was a long time before I realized what this vicious cycle even was; it just seemed like Chris was sick more often than most.

It became more and more common over the years... drink too much, try to stop, get sick, drink some more, drink too much, try to stop, get sick, drink some more, repeat.

When the alcohol was sparse, I'd find him sneaking gobs of pills that he was prescribed from his doctor for depression and anxiety.

Once, I remember seeing him take a handful of pills out of his pants pocket. I asked him what they were and he quickly shoved them into his mouth to swallow them like a tweaked out teenager before I even had a chance to realize what was going on.

I don't know how much you know about Ambien, but it's an extremely potent sleep aid; it doesn't take much to do the trick.

Chris would often take enough Ambien in one sitting to cause him to do things like fall asleep, face first, into his bowl of spaghetti right at the dinner table. Or, drive his brand new Equinox over our mailbox, literally, and then crash it into the side of our house.

There were so many red flags that I mentally bleached pink out of love and inexperience. Looking back on it has me questioning my entire ability to recognize anything amiss. Do you ever feel that way, reader friends? Like, 'How the hell did I miss *that*?'

Don't beat yourself up about it. We just don't know what we don't know. And back then, I clearly didn't know as much about this disease as I thought I did.

I had spent years prior to this watching my sister do all kinds of crazy things because of her addictions. Yet, there I was oblivious to what was going on with my own husband.

You'd think that with my experience with my sister's drug and alcohol addiction, and with the way Chris was behaving it would have been blatantly obvious.

Alcoholism hits differently when it finds its way into your home.

But, when I talked to him, he blamed his behavior on feeling awful about losing his job. And I believed him.

Though innocent, that was a big mistake on my part. Huge. Chris's addiction turned him into a very believable liar. It's scary, really, to think back at how good he was at it.

19

HOSPITALIZATION

S hortly after he lost his job this first go round, Chris had a seizure in the living room in front of our children. This is something my oldest still remembers vividly to this day. He was only five years old when it happened.

I obviously knew that something was severely wrong, but didn't know exactly what. Or, maybe I did and I was somehow suppressing it. I don't honestly know, but this seizure was the beginning of my epiphany.

Chris's seizure was quite a turning point for both of us. It was the (eventual) revealing event in determining that Chris was, in fact, an alcoholic. Though it took some time to figure it all out, this seizure was one of many side effects he was having from a severe detox from alcohol.

He was hospitalized directly from the emergency room to look further into the cause of his seizure. Soon after we got him settled in, a nurse pulled me aside and asked me a question that changed the course of my life forever.

She asked, "Is there any way your husband is an alcoholic or is withdrawing from alcohol? If so, we need to know because it can be very dangerous."

This was part of my 'aha' moment... Kind of. It was the very second that I sorta did, sorta didn't, but should have completely realized that we had a very severe problem on our hands.

The only thing I actually knew for sure in the moment was that this nurse's question was going to really stick with me. And it did.

You see, Chris was still denying his problem and part of me still believed him. Part of me *wanted* to believe him. The alternative was legit frightening, you know?

My response to the nurse was a very weak, 'Maybe?'.

More guilt.

What I wish I would have said screamed was, "Yes! Yessss, please help him! Please help *me!*" But, it hit me in retrospect. Yep... When I look back on this very moment, I think to myself, "Annie, you idiot, *that* was your moment!"

That small part of me that just wasn't sure was trying to protect Chris. When I told him what the nurse asked me he became very upset about it and it all felt too overwhelming and confusing to push it.

What was happening to Chris was embarrassing for him. I don't know if he knew what was really happening or not, but I do know that it wasn't until many years later that he outwardly admitted to me that he even had a drinking problem.

He'd tiptoe around it saying things like, "I know I need to get my shit together," or, "I'm trying to do better," but never an admission of having the disease.

My old insecurities sometimes get me wondering things like: What if keeping my mouth shut when all of this started may be part of why Chris is dead now?

Maybe if I was stronger, maybe if he didn't care so much about what others thought, maybe if *I* didn't care so much about what others thought, maybe if I did beg for more help... Just maybe... He'd be alive and well today.

But, in my heart of hearts, I know better.

I'm part of a group text where a fellow Al-Anon member shares his daily thoughts on recovery. The very same day I sat and wrote this part of my story, my old character flaws were trying to creep in and take away my courage.

I was struggling to write the words that I needed to write. I received these little Godwinks through messages from our group's approved literature just when I needed them:

- "I must remind myself daily that I can save only myself.
- "Whenever I give in to my natural impulse and habit to take over and try to force a change, I'm in trouble again."
- "When faced with other people's destructive attitudes and behavior, I can love their best and never fear their worst."

You see, one of the things I know now is a slogan in the Al-Anon program: 'The three C's'. I didn't cause Chris's alcoholism. I couldn't control it. And, I couldn't cure it.

I didn't cause it.

I couldn't control it.

I couldn't cure it.

I repeat that to myself about a zillion times a week along with the Serenity Prayer. God, Grant me the serenity to accept the things I cannot change, the courage to change the things I can, and the wisdom to know the difference.

I'm aware that most people know this prayer. But, there's some sort of unexplainable magical power this prayer gives to us when we really need it and recite it with purpose.

Don't believe me? Try it for yourself. The next time you find yourself struggling with something painful or difficult, try it. Pause, take a few slow, deep breaths. Pray, say the serenity prayer. Then proceed, and move on with your day.

I think you'll find that little by little, it really starts to help. Sometimes I even shorten it to a quick, "Accept the things you cannot change, Annie," and it really keeps me on track.

Think about what we're asking our higher ups for here. Whether or not your Higher Power is God doesn't really matter... We are asking the powers that be to grant us peace and calmness in times where something unwanted is happening to us that we cannot change. What a beautiful gift.

This is actually a really neat part of the Al-anon program; we each get to define our own Higher Power.

Besides that, wondering if Chris would still be alive today brings up a whole lotta other questions like... If he was still alive today, would he still be drinking and suffering?

Sometimes I also wonder if Chris would still be alive if I allowed him to continue living with us. Our home was his safe place and he deserved to be there.

But then I can't help but flippy floppy my thoughts and emotions and start to wonder if my kids would be as healthy and happy as they are now if he would have stayed.

And... Uh... What about *me*? Would I be as healthy and happy as I am now if he would have stayed? Or, would I even still be here?

The effects of his disease were really starting to take their toll on all of us.

There's no way to ever know the answers to these questions. But, since Chris's passing, I've realized that the 'what ifs' are a prominent symptom of grief.

Sometimes, while all of this craziness was going on, I'd see glimpses of the Chris I married, but all that did was confuse me more. He'd act like his 'normal' self and I'd think to myself... See, he's fine! This is fine, everything's fine! Everything was not fine.

Chris always had one foot in sea, and one on shore - until years later when things started to get completely out of hand, with no turning back.

20

ALCOHOL INDUCED PSYCHOSIS

W hile in the hospital, so many strange and unbelievable things happened to Chris. It's in this moment in my writing that I have to be honest with you about something. It takes an inhuman, Hulk-sized amount of vulnerability to tell a story of alcoholism. Telling the truth is hard because it threatens to put reputations at risk.

It's one thing to tell your own story, revealing the parts of it that you choose to tell, and keeping the rest inside. It's an entirely different thing when telling your story includes telling intense parts of someone else's story.

There's a really thin line between telling the truth and divulging too much. After agonizing about it over and over... And then over and over again, I've decided to tell some of the more personal things that happened to Chris due to his alcoholism.

Chris deserves his entire story to be told. He suffered so greatly for so long, and I can't stop thinking about all those dang what ifs.

What if telling these parts of his shocking, yet meaningful story helps someone else through their battle with alcoholism? What if telling our story helps another family through their similar crisis? What if it saves a life? What if it prevents someone's children from permanently losing their parent like mine lost theirs?

Besides, how can I tell my story if I don't include such details; what would the point of that be?

I hope that anyone reading this understands that these things that happened to Chris were the effects of his disease, and in no way define who he really was as a person.

This disease took his life, but not before it completely destroyed his mental health. And, not before it completely destroyed our family.

On a more personal level, my children will one day grow up wondering what happened. They also deserve to know the full story, and should, as a part of their own healing process.

For so long, they sat and watched this all unfold, too young to understand it, constantly worrying and wondering what was happening to their daddy.

As mentioned before, the statistics are clear about children who grow up in a home with an alcoholic parent. They are at greater risk for addiction themselves in their adult lives. I can only hope that knowing the full story will help them to make different choices in their lives.

It's a hard thought to put down on paper permanently. But Chris's struggles, and his death, very well may be what saves his sons from going down the same destructive path he went down.

To me, Chris's story is one of selflessness, sacrifice, and heroism; it will never be anything but.

So, I'm going to tell my story in its entirety, with complete respect for Chris. I'm telling it for myself and for our children. I'm telling it for Chris. And, I'm telling it for you - who wouldn't be reading this if you didn't need to hear it.

Let's be honest, I'm not a famous author. If anyone is reading this it's because they need to for one reason or another.

As you read these very personal details about my experience of being the wife of an alcoholic, you may find yourself in my shoes. This is my goal in telling such intimate details of our story.

I'm not here with intentions to air out Chris's most difficult life moments, but I can't exactly put my experience into perspective if I don't.

Here goes.

The first night Chris stayed at the hospital, I went home to try to get some sleep. My parents were taking care of our kids, and I remember feeling a sense of relief. Chris was safe in the hospital and I wasn't going to have to deal with any drama, even if just for one night. With my little ones out of the house, I longed for some much needed, uninterrupted sleep.

That was, until I was awoken around 2 o'clock in the morning by the buzzing of my phone. The nighttime nursing staff was calling me, asking me to rush up to the hospital because Chris was hallucinating and was terrified, asking where I was.

Something I know now but didn't know at the time is that, like seizures, hallucinations are a symptom of alcohol detox. Medical professionals officially term this as alcohol induced psychosis.

During alcohol induced psychosis, a person's thoughts and perceptions are disrupted in ways that prevent them from distinguishing between what's real and what's not.

When I got to Chris's hospital room, he looked panicked. He frantically started motioning for me to come sit next to him. As a reminder, at this point in time, I did not yet know that alcohol induced psychosis was even a thing. I didn't even really have confirmation that Chris was an alcoholic. And, even if I had, there was no way for me to know all that alcoholism entailed.

Needless to say, I was really concerned and confused. When I sat down next to him, he whispered into my ear that we needed to escape the hospital immediately because the staff was hiding dead babies and burning them in the basement.

Realizing very quickly that he wasn't in his right state of mind, I talked him into staying overnight, promising him we would figure things out in the morning.

I know what you're thinking... How do you talk someone into ignoring something like dead babies in the basement of a hospital until morning?

Well, it actually helped that Chris wasn't in a healthy state of mind, and he trusted me. I felt good about calming him and was hopeful for a restful night and new beginning in the morning.

He fell asleep and I laid by his side trying to process what was happening. I felt overwhelmingly worried for my husband as well as for myself and our kids. To put it mildly, it's excruciating to see your spouse in such a state. I didn't know I had so many tears to cry.

This was the second really hard situation I found myself in as a young adult - even harder than what Sam had put me through with his affair. I was now thirty-one years old and already finding myself in another super convoluted and excruciating situation.

This hardship was much sadder for me. It gave me a whole new, and much more heartbreaking, definition of terrified than what I experienced during my first marriage.

Unfortunately, the next morning things were the opposite of much better. After researching it years later, I learned that alcohol induced psychosis generally lasts a few days.

Chris woke up in another panic, jumped out of bed, and started running around the hospital hallway in nothing but his gown - barefoot and ass out.

He had no idea where he was or even that he was running around almost naked. This is definitely not something that Chris would do, even in his right state of mind.

He even ran into the patient's room across the hall marked hazardous for C. Diff. It was a huge ordeal with a lot of commotion from the nurses.

When hospital staff tried to get Chris back to his room, he made a break for it. He took off down the stairwell and escaped outside. I ran after him, screaming his name, begging him to stop. He just kept telling me to follow him, motioning me along with his flailing arms.

Once we were all the way outside in a parking lot, Chris stopped and I pleaded with him to go back inside. He was standing there in his gown, questioning me about why I'd want to go back into a place that was hiding dead babies and burning them in the basement.

I had no answer for that. I mean, what could I even say to argue my point? He was absolutely sure that the hospital was doing this horrible thing and that I thought it was okay. He was just as sure that there were dead babies in the hospital basement as I was that there weren't.

By the grace of God, as Chris and I stood there together in the parking lot, arguing about the nonexistent dead babies, a police officer drove up to us and very kindly and gently asked Chris if he needed help.

To this day, I don't know if the hospital staff called the police for help, or if the universe knew I was desperate for help and placed this officer in the right place at the right time.

Chris told the officer about the dead babies being hidden in the basement and, much to my surprise, the officer offered to help him, explaining that he would make sure to look into it.

He was able to get Chris into his squad car, back to his hospital room, and strapped to the bed, sedated.

I was very grateful for the way this officer treated Chris with respect and took care of him with such empathy. That entire situation could have ended very differently.

When Chris came to, they brought him to get a few scans as they were still trying to officially determine the cause of his seizure. All I can think now, is how stupid it was of me to not have listened more carefully to the nurse who seemed to know what was happening to him the entire time.

The nurse allowed me to walk next to Chris's stretcher as they wheeled him to where he needed to be. I was standing on his left as we went on our way. Where I was standing probably wouldn't be something someone would remember as a significant detail of a trip through the hospital corridors, but for me, it was.

Tattooed very vividly into my thoughts was Chris turning his head to the right to tell our youngest son, "Daddy's going to be okay, [Buddy], I promise."

Our son wasn't at the hospital that day. Sadly, Chris's disease didn't allow him to follow through on that promise.

I don't have a lump in my throat right now, you do. Ugh, you guys! I'm gonna have to sneak in another really tough truth here... Some things just cannot be erased from your brain.

The nurse gently placed her cold hand on mine as tears were rolling down my face. She didn't say anything to me, but her touch was her way of comforting me and saying she felt badly for what I was going through.

She could tell that I was terrified, I'm sure.

After we dropped Chris off at his destination, she finally said something to me that has never left my heart. She told me she could tell how much I loved Chris because 'patients like him' weren't normally accompanied in the hospital by anyone.

Though she meant well, this was not very comforting to hear. It frightened me even more, making me wonder what was in store for Chris and our little family. Lord only knew that what was in store would be a zillion times worse than anything I could have ever predicted.

A few other concerning things happened with Chris during that hospital stay. When we returned back to his room after his tests were complete, he took the brush out of my purse and waved it around doing magical Harry Potter spells and calling people Muggles. Chris was a jokester, but this wasn't something he was doing to be funny.

I had to make a decision on what to do next and was advised by the psychiatrist on staff to send Chris to stay on the seventh floor of the hospital. This was the mental health unit on the psychiatric floor.

At that point, I really didn't feel like I had much of a choice. I reluctantly signed the paperwork for him, as his Power of Attorney, and he was whisked off to the seventh floor almost immediately.

By his third day there, I was finally able to visit him during their very strict visitation hours. He had fully detoxed by then, so when I saw him he was back to his normal self. He was also very unhappy with me. He was almost completely unaware of what had happened in the previous days.

Chris was on lockdown for his own safety, miserable, confused and livid with me for having him held there. Once I signed him in, I signed away all rights for either of us to change our minds; he had to stay for the entire seven days.

I went to visit him every day he was there, even on days when he wasn't allowed to have visitors. I felt responsible for him and was extremely anxious and worried. Somehow, sitting in that waiting room felt like I was supporting him. It was the closest thing I could do to actually being there for him.

I distinctly remember visiting him on the Fourth of July. I sat with him in the family room for the one hour I was allowed to - along with the other patients and their visitors. The nursing staff passed out a special treat to celebrate the holiday, chocolate cake and juice to the patients and their loved ones. It felt very elementary school. And since Chris had fully detoxed and was sober at the time, it also felt very wrong for him to be there. I tried to remind myself of what had just occurred in the previous weeks and asked him to please do whatever it was that the doctors were asking him to do before I left him there that night.

I very desperately wanted this hospital stay to be the fix to all of our problems. I had hope that Chris would magically become himself again. How naive of me.

I watched fireworks through my car window on the drive home from the hospital. Which made me even sadder because that was something we always did as a family. Instead, Chris was in the hospital, my kids were with my parents, and I was all by myself, feeling empty and scared.

Chris never forgave me for putting him in the 'psych ward'. Even years later when we would get into it about this or that, he'd remind me angrily that I once had him locked into 'the loony bin' because I 'thought he was a crazy person'.

More guilt.

During that hospital stay, Chris was diagnosed by the psychiatrist on staff with general personality disorder and bipolar disorder. But, over time, I learned he was neither of those things; he was an alcoholic.

This psychiatrist was no longer taking on new patients, however, explained to the both of us that he wanted to bring Chris onto his caseload. He saw potential in him and wanted to try to help our family.

I was, and still am, very grateful for doctors like this. I attended all of Chris's appointments with him in order to be kept in the loop and to be sure he was being truthful.

At the time, accompanying Chris to his appointments felt like the right thing to do, but in reality it was just another attempted form of me trying to control the situation. You know, being sure he went and told the truth and all.

Misdiagnosis occurred because Chris wasn't entirely truthful when he talked to the psychiatrist in the hospital. I was determined to prevent any future lies. I'll give you one guess on how well that worked out for me.

Though lying to medical professionals was a definite pattern for Chris, I'm not entirely sure he was even able to be truthful. I mean honestly, he literally just thought he was a magical wizard at Hogwarts.

We were both terrified and struggling to know what to do or how to answer questions.

The seven days that Chris was held on the psychiatric floor were very difficult for both of us. I felt very alone, confused, and isolated. And, I can only imagine he was feeling much the same.

Phew. Are we still taking deep breaths?

V

DADDY'S SICK

"A little voice came on the phone and said, 'Daddy when you comin' home?'

He said the first thing that came to his mind:

I'm already there. Take a look around. I'm the sunshine in your hair. I'm the shadow on the ground. I'm the whisper in the wind and I'll be there 'til the end. Can you feel the love we share?

Oh, I'm already there."

— LONESTAR, I'M ALREADY THERE

Though I wish I did, I didn't have the power to hope big enough, pray Chris's pain and alcoholism away, or beg it all to just freaking stop. I only knew that I could not continue to try to raise these babies all by myself with the added obstacles that Chris was bringing to our lives.

21

HARD TRUTH

ALCOHOLISM WEARS CAMOUFLAGE LIKE IT'S GOING OUT OF STYLE.

Hey friend, I gotta tell ya, alcoholism hides. It's extremely good at it too, making everyone in its presence wonder if they are really seeing what they're seeing.

Alcoholism is manipulative, it tricks people, and it often mimics other illnesses - like depression, bipolar disorder and general personality disorder, for example.

Chris wasn't bipolar and he didn't have a personality disorder. He was medicated for both diagnoses, but he was not either of the two. It's entirely possible that your loved one who is struggling has some hidden symptoms too.

After we returned home from this hospital stay, Chris's drinking and lies continued unfortunately, but this time more in hiding. I caught him in so many lies and finally decided that I had no choice but to ask him to leave our home. This was the first of two times I had to resort to doing this throughout our ten year marriage.

Of course it wasn't what I wanted to do; however I was realizing quickly that I didn't have any control over what Chris did or didn't do.

I wasn't yet strong enough to know my own worth, but I did have a strong, primal, motherly need to protect my children from the trauma we were experiencing. I am their mother, and at the time, was their only safe place. Remember, my oldest son's dad was MIA at this time as well.

I was hopeful that, in asking Chris to leave, he would realize how much he needed to/wanted to/should clean up his act and return to his family - changed and healthy.

There I was trying to control things again... And it actually worked that time. Temporarily. Chris stopped drinking and started going to AA meetings.

Although, going to AA meetings was short lived for Chris. He was, from what I could tell, able to stay sober for the next five years or so with just a few bumps in the road along the way. He moved back in with us within a month after I asked him to leave this first time.

Chris never 'worked' an AA program for long. He said it 'wasn't for him'. In my opinion, knowing him as well as I did, 'It's not for me' meant... It's too painful to go so I'm not.

Since my sister was also a long-time drug addict and alcoholic, I knew it was imperative for Chris to attend AA meetings and 'work a program'. This really is the only way to work on one's recovery successfully, but when I tried forcing him to go, he'd leave the house and end up at a bar instead.

For a while; however, he seemed to have the ability to stop himself from drinking. I say 'seemed to' because nobody ever really knows except the alcoholic themself.

For the next five years, life was okay. We had the okayest life we could have. I mean, things weren't exactly amazing and fantastic, but hey, anydamnthing was better than the craziness we were living in prior. Life was fairly mundane, but good as far as raising kids and living without drama goes.

We sold our home and purchased a new one in the small town in which I teach. Chris got a new, stable nine-to-five and life continued - as it does.

For a while, our children were happy and thriving. Chris and I weren't very close as far as marriages go, but he was trying to be healthy and I was determined to make things work. There was always a lot of love and care between us in spite of all of our issues.

In order to do that, I tried to be understanding of how he was feeling. I wasn't always good at it, but I did try. I began to focus my efforts on my own healing and taking care of the kids.

~~Guilt, guilt, guilt~~. This was the beginning of my own journey toward healing and recovery.

I would describe our relationship at this point as cohabitation and friendship. We were a pretty good parenting team; I often referred to us as a well-oiled machine.

There were just no more sparks or fireworks between Chris and I. I think we had just been through too much at that point and neither of us were working a program to help us along the way.

As time ticked on, fast forward five years or so, Chris started acting strangely again. Our children also started having drastic reactions to the dynamics in our home. They weren't babies anymore, so this time I noticed a clear change in their behavior as well.

Our oldest son started to withdraw from his relationship with Chris, while our youngest started to become overly attached.

Our little one started to feel extremely anxious when he wasn't with his dad, especially when having to go to school. His therapist called it an 'unhealthy attachment'.

Only seven years old at the time, he would say things like, "Daddy is sick, Mommy, that's why you're fighting. He loves you. Don't be mad at him."

'Daddy's sick' is something I had to tell the kids often when Chris wasn't acting like himself. Or was passed out on the couch in the basement. Or wouldn't be seen upstairs for days at a time.

The entire two years prior to Chris's death had been difficult on us all to say the least. The drinking started back up, at some point, and we started fighting pretty often.

The complication comes in when, after ten years of dealing with the drama of alcoholism, it becomes unclear who the person even is anymore. As the years pass by, it gets harder and harder to decipher who the 'real' person is underneath the many costumes alcohol puts on them.

In my best Annie explanation, all I can do is just say Chris just wasn't the same person he used to be. It no longer mattered if he was actively drinking or not. He was in pain. That pain manifested itself as anger and irritability, and he started blaming everyone else for anything that went wrong.

By this time, it was like the Chris we knew and loved was already gone. Our family has grieved the loss of this beautiful soul twice now.

In case anyone is wondering, Yes, I'm sitting here bawling, typing that. Fucking Ouch.

22

TOO MUCH HOLIDAY CHEER

T hanksgiving of 2018, the last Thanksgiving the boys and I ever spent with Chris, was a tumultuous one.

Sigh, I have so many regrets about this particular night.

I've endured two more Thanksgivings since this last one I had with Chris, the first when he was in rehab and the second when we were visiting him at the cemetery. Both years, I found myself wishing that final Thanksgiving with him had played out differently.

By that, I specifically mean I wish I would have treated Chris with more empathy that day. I'm more aware of a few things now than I was back then. First, of his inability to control what he was doing, and second, of my ability to control how I handled each situation that arose between us.

I try to give myself some grace in knowing that I was always just doing the best I could.

But, like... I feel like the biggest piece of shit on the planet that I was more mad at him than worried about him that day - on Thanksgiving of all days.

Deeeep sigh. I know I have to give myself grace and forgive myself as I try to do the same with Chris. I'm still processing through a lot of that, and, I'm pretty sure that's going to be a lifelong process.

That evening, I was upstairs in my kitchen cleaning up when I heard a cacophony of repetitive tumbling, groaning, and a final booming thud.

Chris had just walked past me in the kitchen moments before, so I knew that he had fallen down the stairs. When I ran to the top of the steps, I looked down and saw him, bloody and struggling to stay conscious.

It was one of those moments that plays out in slow motion. My body movements seemed to go at a snail's pace, but my mind was going a million miles a minute. Oh my gosh, is he okay? Is he drunk? WTF happened? Is he drunk? His head actually went through the wall. Holy shit, he's bleeding... Wait, is he drunk?

By the time Chris became alert again, his face was already starting to show visible bruising. Chris plummeted so rapidly that his head put a giant hole in the wall at the bottom of the stairs. He was lucky scrapes and bruises were his only injuries.

A stud was just a few centimeters away from where his head penetrated the drywall. It was visible from the destruction and I hate to think what would have happened to him that evening if he landed just a smidge to the right.

When I asked Chris what happened, he explained that he was holding his dog, Skeeter, as he walked down the stairs. At some point, Skeeter tried jumping from his arms, and as Chris went to catch him he tripped and tumbled down the steps.

Chris's story may sound like a believable one, but active alcoholics are liars. I know that is a gigantic blanket statement, but... Ummm... Active alcoholics are liars. And Chris was no exception.

Anyone who knew Skeeter would know that this was a clear lie. Skeeter was a dachshund with a bad back. That dog lived in Chris's arms and actually required being held when going up and down the stairs. Skeeter just wouldn't try to leap out of Chris's arms.

It may sound super insensitive to label all alcoholics as any one thing, but here's the deal... That word 'active' is important. Alcoholics who are actively drinking lie all.the.time. Recovering alcoholics may be a different story.

Look dear readers, I'm not telling you anything you don't already know. I'm also not telling this story to prove to anyone how much Chris lied. I'm telling it because I've been carrying around an extremely heavy bag of guilt about this night since it happened and it's time to reveal another hard truth.

23

HARD TRUTH

YOU, TOO, ARE SICK FROM THIS DISEASE.

I knew I was being lied to and I was over it. Because I was also sick from this family disease, I was unable to control my emotions and became frustrated with Chris instead of empathetic.

We got into a screaming match. I shouted at him, while blood was dripping from the cuts in his head, saying that I didn't appreciate him sitting at the Thanksgiving table telling everyone he was thankful for me, his 'amazing wife', when he clearly wasn't.

It wasn't exactly my shining moment, friends.

This man just fell down the stairs and hurt himself badly. And I was yelling at him. At the time, I felt justified in my actions. Now that I have a lot of self-recovery under my belt, I can see that in these really tough and frustrating moments, I completely misunderstood this disease and stole Chris's worth as a human being right out from under him.

This is something I've fought a personal battle with every single day since before Chris even passed away. His death certainly has heightened my feelings of guilt and shame because... Well, I can no longer make amends with him about it face to face.

It may be difficult for anyone else to understand my frustration with Chris over this incident. I didn't really even understand it myself until my therapist asked me why I reacted the way that I did.

It isn't like I told myself to get angry that day. I just also didn't tell myself not to - that's where my mistake happened.

To answer my therapist's question, this fall was a giant wake up call for me; it was one of my first (and correct) inklings that Chris was, in fact, drinking again.

And that, my friends, ripped my whole entire heart right out of my chest because I knew exactly what that meant. This wasn't our first rodeo.

The very moment this all happened, I knew that I was in for another extremely difficult, extremely scary, extremely painful round of Chris's alcoholism. So I became uncontrollably and overwhelmingly angry with him.

He made me feel pretty bad about focusing on my feelings instead of him at a time when he had just been hurt badly. He had every right to feel that way. Alcoholic or not, Chris was a human being. One that I loved and cared for, and I was not treating him as such.

Part of my personal recovery is doing that thing called making amends. This is also a part of an alcoholic's recovery process. We make amends in order to move forward from wrongs we've made in our past.

Since I no longer get to make amends with Chris about any of the ways I wronged him during our time on this earth together, I'm left fighting some really tough battles inside myself. This adds quite a bit of complexity to my healing. It means I have to make amends to *myself* about it. Which, like... Feels a thousand times harder.

I'm finding that, for me personally, it's much easier to forgive other people than it is to forgive myself.

You may have noticed that I keep calling alcoholism a family disease. On top of that, alcoholism is also a very complicated disease. The word itself warns us all: dis-ease. Not only does it completely infiltrate the alcoholic's life, it also wrecks havoc on their entire family:

"Alcoholism is a family disease. Compulsive drinking affects the drinker and it affects the drinker's relationships. Friendships, employment, childhood, parenthood, love affairs, and marriages all suffer from the effects of alcoholism. Those special relationships in which a person is really close to an alcoholic are affected most, and we who care are the most caught up in the behavior of another person. We react to an alcoholic's behavior. Seeing that the drinking is out of hand, we try to control it. We are ashamed of the public scenes but try to handle it in private. It isn't long before we feel we are to blame and take the hurts, the fears, and the guilt of an alcoholic. We too, become ill."

— HOW AL-ANON WORKS

That night, when Chris came upstairs to go to sleep, I was jolted awake to another loud crash. He had fallen again. This time, I wasn't sure if it was because he was drunk or because he was disoriented from the first fall. Honestly, it was probably a little of column A and a little of column B.

He hit his already injured face on the nightstand next to the bed and refused to let me take him to the emergency room. I laid awake the rest of the night crying and making sure he was still breathing while he slept on a blood soaked pillow.

The next day, we agreed that he needed to go to the emergency room. He was concerned about 'what to say' to the doctors. I told him to simply tell the truth - Skeeter leaped out of his arms and he fell down the stairs trying to catch him. Right?

For some reason that I'm not sure I'll ever understand, when he went to the emergency room, he lied to them about what happened as well - with an entirely different lie. He told them that he got hit in the face with an elbow while playing basketball.

I only know this because one of the ER nurses was an acquaintance that we saw at our son's basketball game that same day. She jokingly asked if Chris was done with his basketball career yet and I fake laughed along with them as he stumbled through his lie of a response to her.

This fall was the beginning of the end of our marriage. More disturbingly, it was also the beginning of the end of Chris's life. Chris was never able to gain back control of his alcoholism from that point on.

I don't know why holidays always seemed to amp things up with Chris's struggles. I hate that I've had to relive this very sad memory every Thanksgiving since this last one we spent together, and I'm hoping I can make peace with it so that isn't a tradition I continue for myself from here on out.

My family has a beautiful holiday tradition where anyone who attends our Thanksgiving meal signs their name on the fabric tablecloth from our dinner table. My mom then stitches over the signatures with thread to make them a permanent reminder of Thanksgivings of the past.

Seeing Chris's signature in multiple places on our tablecloth at our Thanksgiving meal this past year was both a blessing and a condemnation of sorts. It's a reminder of some truly beautiful memories we had as a family, as well as a painful reminder, a hammered in nail, of how fragile life really is; a reminder that there will always be an empty seat at our Thanksgiving table where Chris used to be.

I've learned the hard way that it is so very important to not just be thankful for all of our blessings on special holidays, but every day, even the really ugly ones.

On Christmas Eve, just a few weeks after this Thanksgiving incident, I woke up in the middle of the night because I had forgotten to move the dang Elf on the Shelf.

I went down to the basement where the elf was still sitting from the previous night. Chris was up late playing video games per usual when I saw him quickly slide something under the couch cushion.

This was a classic Chris move so I knew what that something was. I can vividly remember more times than I can count on my fingers that Chris pulled this not so smooth move when I entered a room.

I took it upon myself to go remove that vodka bottle from under the couch cushion even though I knew doing so would only do one thing - hurt me.

I silently walked past Chris, setting the vodka bottle on the coffee table next to the couch, and went upstairs. All of our family's Christmas gifts were sitting beautifully underneath our tree. The boys were sleeping soundly, with dreams of sugarplums dancing in their heads, and I was balled up in the middle of the living room floor, bawling.

Chris came up to talk to me and instead of screaming at him like I wanted to, I simply asked him to not say a word to me about it because doing so had substantial potential to ruin all future Christmases for our family.

I then placed the elf onto a branch of the glowing Christmas tree for the boys, went to my bedroom, and locked the door. Chris knocked on the door a few times, begging me to talk to him, but I didn't answer.

I couldn't. I knew I wouldn't be able to control my rage and the repercussions of that had the ability to be permanently damaging. We'd get into another screaming match and I couldn't risk the boys waking up to that in the middle of the night, ever... But especially on such a memorable holiday for them. Can you imagine *that* being one of their childhood Christmas Eve memories?

These two holiday occurrences made it clear. We were deep into Chris's alcoholism again. Fast forward through almost another year of living through this disease after that... And that's when I found myself standing next to that train...

24

ANOTHER JOB LOST

Then, in October of 2019, Chris lost his job for the second time. It's crazy how the universe works. It almost feels like when I was too scared to pull the trigger myself on making a big change in our lives, the universe made a big change for me.

During this time, I was obvi a hot mess ball of anxiety and worry. The financial stress amongst all the other stressors felt really impossible to handle. Plus, now I could see my kids both starting to really struggle with it all as well.

When I wanted to take the boys to fun places, Chris stopped coming along. Our youngest preferred to stay home with his dad, our oldest always went with me.

I remember asking our little one to go to a pumpkin farm right before Halloween. I thought he'd want to pick a pumpkin to carve for the upcoming holiday. He said he wanted to stay home to "help take care of Daddy."

When our oldest son and I returned home, I found Chris passed out next to one of his 'water bottles' of vodka while our youngest son sat on his lap watching YouTube videos. It was a sight I won't soon forget.

Not only was I livid with Chris for putting our child through this, but I was also upset with myself for leaving him home alone with his dad. Something I knew I no longer should have been doing. Just as I had made the decision that he wasn't allowed to drive the kids anywhere anymore either.

25

DOMESTIC VIOLENCE

The next morning, we had one of two physical altercations in our marriage. One happened much earlier on in our marriage during the first go round of the chaos.

If you know either of us personally, you know physical altercations are uncharacteristic for both of us. No one would ever think that anything like this would be possible between us. Physical altercations are an extremely unfortunate symptom of alcoholism.

Before I go into details on these two incidents I think it's important to note a few things. Alcoholism has a way of making everyone involved feel a little batshit crazy, whether it's the alcoholic themself or the spouse of the alcoholic.

There is no excuse for this type of behavior. Ever. It's inappropriate, scary, dangerous, shameful and can really generate some lasting effects on each person's psyche.

However, when you're in the midst of such a crisis, you find yourself in situations you never even thought imaginable.

According to the National Institute on Alcohol Abuse and Alcoholism, domestic violence is one of the most common problems that arise between spouses when one partner abuses alcohol. (NIAAA)

The World Health Organization defines intimate partner violence as any behavior within an intimate relationship that causes physical, psychological or sexual harm to those in that relationship. It includes acts of physical aggression like slapping, hitting, kicking or beating, psychological abuse - [such as] intimidation, constant belittling or humiliation, and forced sexual intercourse. [It also includes] any other controlling behavior like isolating a person from family and friends, monitoring their movements and restricting access to information or assistance. (World Health Organization)

In the article titled 'Intimate Partner Violence and Alcohol', the WHO explains that alcohol consumption, especially at harmful and hazardous levels, is a major contributor to the occurrence of intimate partner violence, with various links between the two. (World Health Organization)

Chris awoke and came to me with a hug as an apology, but I had had enough; I just couldn't bring myself to feel anything other than indignation. Martyr much, Annie? He wouldn't let go of me, so I started punching his arms over and over again to make him let me go. His arms were bruised up the next day.

I can't even put into words how awful I feel about how this went down. Ultimately, this interaction was the deciding factor in me asking him to leave our family home. Things had gone way too far out of control and I needed this drama to just stop.

Clearly, this is another instance where I wish I could make amends with Chris. I have a lot of shame and guilt surrounding this incident in particular, along with another physical altercation we got into many years before.

In desperation for change toward the beginning of our marriage, I had once started bringing all of Chris's belongings out of the house and into the garage because I wanted him to take his dysfunction and get out of my life. This happened right after I found him drinking after his first hospital stay.

He was drunk again and started angrily demanding me to stop moving his things out. I refused, so he grabbed me around the waist to try to stop me. I started flailing around, trying to break free when my sweatshirt went over my head.

A combination of me breathing heavily from energy exertion and my sweatshirt blocking airflow caused me to collapse. We both hit the ground and apparently my hand hit the wall at some point. I'm pretty sure my thumb was broken, but I never went to the hospital for fear of domestic violence charges on either of us.

Yikes. That is not something I've ever told anyone except my therapist.

I know how crazy that all has to sound to anyone reading this right now.

It

was

crazy!

As Chris became sicker and sicker, I also became sicker and sicker. Our relationship became toxic and turbulent. Neither of us was handling life very well at this point and I knew that it was time to do something I had been dreading for a very long time.

VI

SELFISH OR SELF-LOVING?

"Life is amazing. And then it's awful. And then it's amazing again. And in between the amazing and the awful it's ordinary and mundane and routine. Breathe in the amazing, hold on through the awful, and relax and exhale during the ordinary. That's just living heartbreaking, soul-healing, amazing, awful, ordinary life. And it's breathtakingly beautiful. "

— LR KNOST

On October 27, 2019, shortly after I peeled myself away from those tempting train tracks, I excruciatingly asked my husband to leave our family home. There was no way for me to know then that he would be found dead within a year after that.

The guilt is strong with this one.

This decision was both extremely difficult in some ways, yet extremely simple in others. Yes, you read that correctly... In part, it was extremely simple to ask my husband to move out.

Living in that kind of utter chaos for an entire decade yanked the complication right out of my decision.

I should probably pause here for a little necessary disclaimer. This part of my story is going to upset some people that don't fully understand this disease. And, by upset I mean infuriate.

I'm well aware of this and though it isn't my intention, I simply refuse to skip over difficult parts of my story in order to avoid others' hard feelings.

I've been told on more than one occasion that I abandoned Chris when he needed me the most. It's these types of ideals that silence those of us that are stuck between a rock and a hard place while battling on the front lines with an alcoholic; we're damned if we do and we're damned if we don't.

I want to note something for anyone reading this who is struggling to find their own voice: A need for comfort shouldn't take precedence over a need for the type of healing and growth that only the truth can provide.

Gallantly standing up for what's right, especially when the rest of the world wants you to sit down and shut up, is something to be proud of. Sometimes we have to be brave, find our strength, and take chances.

It's important to own our stories, unapologetically.

You see, owning our truths and refusing to sit quietly is a triumph that changes our trajectory toward the next level in healing. It's the only way to move forward toward a more peaceful life. As the saying goes, 'Nothing changes if nothing changes.'

This is my story. I have every right to tell it in its entirety, with full authenticity, and that's exactly what I intend to do. I plan to scream it, actually... Without hiding behind a fear for what others may think.

I used to pity myself, lacking the confidence I needed to stand my ground. I'm no longer that scared young girl; no longer a victim of the privations of life. The new me is a brave woman filled with confidence and purpose - thanks to all the growth my hardships forced me into.

When Chris left, he went to his dad's house, which was his childhood home. His dad's house was always jam packed full of 'stuff' every time I visited there throughout our marriage.

This gave Chris no comfortable space to live. He texted often, describing his dad's house as hoarded, but honestly he didn't need to. I knew what he was going into when he left our home. I had been there many times before.

He was very vocal with me about how little space he had, how uncomfortable it felt, and how living that way didn't give him a healing environment. And, yet, I still believed this was the best decision for everyone involved.

~~More guilt.~~ More chances for me to practice being strong and brave. More grace to learn to give myself. More breaths to breathe.

26

ALCOHOLISM IS A REAL DISEASE

M any times throughout this book, you'll notice me calling alcoholism a disease. Knowing that alcoholism is a disease, begs a really important followup question: How is alcoholism a disease?

Doesn't the drinker have a choice in whether or not they pick up that bottle of beer or booze? Can't they just choose not to drive to the liquor store? Cancer is a disease; people suffering from cancer don't have a choice.

Umpf... The answer to this is heavily debated and quite complicated.

For me personally, I know it's a disease because it fucking killed my husband. It started in his brain and then it infiltrated his entire body.

So, yeah, it's not difficult for me to look at alcoholism as a disease, specifically a mental health disease. Though, with full disclosure, it used to be harder for me to understand.

It also helps me to look at alcoholism as a gateway disease to other long-term health risks. Over time, excessive alcohol use can lead to the development of chronic diseases and other serious problems, including alcohol use disorder and problems with learning, memory, and mental health.

Chronic health conditions that have been linked to excessive alcohol use include:

- High blood pressure, heart disease, and stroke
- Liver disease
- Digestive problems
- Learning and memory problems
- Mental health problems including anxiety and depression
- Cancer

Center for Disease Control

As you're reading this, you may be wondering a few things. Since alcoholism is a disease, doesn't that mean Chris was sick? And, if so, then how could you kick him out of your home?

It's time for another hard truth.

27

HARD TRUTH

SOMETIMES WE HAVE TO DETACH, WITH LOVE, IN ORDER TO SURVIVE.

I'm sure you've heard the old adage, 'You can only harm me if I allow you to.' Though spoken often, there is a real and deep truth to such a simple phrase.

Whenever feelings of guilt and shame pop into my thoughts, I have to always remind myself that if I would have kept living the way I was, I would probably have ended up dead myself.

And if I didn't make it out of this alive, our children would have lost both of their parents. Can you even imagine that? A double fatality caused by the destruction of alcoholism. There was, unfortunately, no stopping Chris's death, but I still had a lot of life left in me.

BIG, UNCOMFORTABLE CHANGES
WILL HAVE TO BE MADE

I had been living with Chris and his alcoholism for ten years by the time I built up enough courage to ask him to leave. Living with a person who struggles with addiction is a buy one, get one free situation... One is never far apart from the other.

So then you may be wondering, what the straw was that broke the camel's back, after dealing with it for so many years. Easy. Chris's alcoholism had started affecting the rest of us in the house in scary ways; his behaviors were wreaking havoc on all of our lives.

Writing the words 'wrecking havoc' doesn't really even scratch the surface of the actual chaos we were living in. Wreaking havoc feels a lot like a sugar coat.

Just in case you're finding yourself in the same boat, trying to decide what you should do next... I want to just say a couple things to you that might help you make your decision.

First, if and when the time is right for you to make an uncomfortable change, you'll know. If you don't know, then the time may not be right; our instincts are usually pretty effective at being a guiding light.

Second, the decision you ultimately make *is* the right decision; decisions made are always decisions that were supposed to be made - even when they feel difficult. Though it's really hard, try not to doubt yourself.

Before making this big, uncomfortable change in our home, you better believe I researched the long term effects on children who have an alcoholic parent. It goes without saying, I learned some really alarming things:

- Alcoholism runs in families
  - Male children of alcoholics are four times more likely to become an alcoholic themselves
    - Perpetuating the cycle of family pain on other generations
  - Daughters of alcoholics are three times more likely to become an alcoholic themselves
    - Perpetuating the cycle of family pain on other generations

- ○ Children of alcoholics who don't become an alcoholic themselves, are more likely to marry one
  - You get the idea
- Children of alcoholics are more likely to abuse alcohol and other drugs
  - Yep
- Children of alcoholics are more likely to have problems in school
- Life in an alcoholic family is often characterized by pain, guilt, fear, tension, and insecurity

Centers for Disease Control

I asked Chris to leave our home because I had to protect my children. It was a difficult decision. I loved and cared about my husband deeply. Besides that, I was worried about him; he was very sick.

My children were starting to show many worrisome signs of trauma: outbursts of anger, throwing up from fear and distress, not wanting to go to school, and a general sense of unease and anxiety.

Their therapist made it clear to me that they were both susceptible to the long-term effects of having an alcoholic parent, highlighting that the only way to give them a shot at a normal adulthood was to get them out of the situation.

~~See? I didn't have a choice! I had to make this difficult decision for my children. I worried about their welfare along with Chris's.~~

~~Chris's behaviors were affecting them negatively and they were going to continue to do so unless I made a drastic change. I couldn't control what he was choosing to do, but I wasn't completely powerless. I had a decision to make and I made it.~~

~~My kids deserve a safe place to live. All kids do. That's a no brainer. They had been exposed to the mayhem for ten years already. That's basically their *entire* lives. Enough was enough.~~

~~Here's another truth for you. There comes a time when you may have to decide if it's more detrimental for the alcoholic parent to be around or not.~~

Look friends, everything I crossed out is absolutely, unequivocally true. Scratching it out doesn't negate any of it. I slashed through it because I have something big to say, and I needed to prove a point.

I think it's pretty understandable that, as a mom, I wanted to protect my children; not from their dad, but from his disease. Protecting their children is what moms do.

Out of fear of further judgement, I've always told everyone that I made the decisions I made in order to protect my children. But that's only a half truth.

You see, the other half of the truth is not as well received; it's something that a lot of people don't want to hear. 'Protecting the kids' is a reason that makes sense to most. Or, most can at least wrap their brains around it.

HARD TRUTH
YOU. FUCKING. MATTER.

B ut, here's the thing... Are you ready for this giant revelation, friends? Your needs matter.

Whoa, right?

A big part of why I asked Chris to leave our home was because I had to protect myself. I didn't want to live with an alcoholic anymore.

When I've said things like that out loud in the past, it has prompted some people to call me selfish and throw their own insecurities at me like:

"Chris didn't want this divorce. He gave up the moment you kicked him out."

— CHRIS'S DAD

Inhale.

Exhale.

Repeat.

If you ask me, that was spoken like a person who was truly in the deep trenches of the denial stage of grief. So, I try not to take it too personally; however, those words fucking hurt. A lot.

Saying that to me had one goal and one goal only: Blame. And it makes it seem like I *wanted* to divorce Chris, or that it was *my* fault he 'gave up', or that he even gave up in the first place.

Chris didn't give up.

He was in detox when he died for goodness sake; this disease killed him while he was trying to stop drinking (probably for his kids). If he wanted to give up, there were so many other ways to do it other than sit in the insurmountable amount of pain detox puts people through. End of story.

Chris didn't want to be an alcoholic. I mean, I feel like it's safe to say that zero percent of people want to be alcoholics. But, if anyone knew Chris, it was me. I can confidently say that he most certainly did not want to leave his sons without their father.

Sigh, Chris's dad clearly just doesn't understand this disease, and there isn't anything I can do to change that. Insert silent Serenity Prayer here, "Annie, accept the things you cannot change..." But, like, what type of accusation wizardry bullshit is that?

I promise you, guys, I do not have the type of magical power that would be required to cause someone to give up on anything in life - whether it's alcohol or their favorite color or pizza toppings. Big revelation here... If I did, I would have used it to get Chris to stop drinking many moons ago.

I want to remind anyone reading this that I'm not here to defend myself or my choices. I'm here to use my experience to help others understand and deal with the absolute devastation of this disease.

I learned very quickly that when someone dies suddenly and unexpectedly, a few things happen that blindside you. One of those things is called - you get accused of killing that person by means of action or inaction. The spouse of the alcoholic is in a lose, lose situation; we either 'do too much' or 'didn't do enough'.

Even though Chris's death certificate determined his official cause of death a 'heart attack due to prolonged use of alcohol', his father, my ex husband, and his college friends all claim that I killed him.

Chris's dad doesn't get to blame me for his death. Nor does anyone else who has blamed me - and there's been a few; even Chris hinted at it a time or two.

"I feel like everything I love has been taken from me, it's really hard to care anymore."

— CHRIS, JUST SIX DAYS BEFORE HE
DIED

Annnd I'm crying again.

Deepest breaths ever.

At the end of the day, their accusations are what prompted me to start writing this book. So, I can't be entirely mad at it.

I'm mentally strong enough and emotionally healthy enough nowadays to know better than to let their own insecurities seep in. I know this disease well; this disease *lived* in my home with me for ten long years. These accusers can't say the same, so really, their opinions don't carry much weight.

Sadly, when people start playing the blame game to make themselves feel better, it can still hit the strongest and most determined souls brutally. For a brief moment in time, I really started to question myself and my decisions even more so than I already was.

Y'all, as ridiculous as that sounds, I have to be fully transparent with you here... On my difficult days, I sometimes think my accusers are right. I guess it's a good thing that I'm in recovery and my hard days are few and far in between.

The last thing I need is others blaming me for something I had no control over. I beat myself up enough already for every tiny little thing I ever 'did wrong' and every single mean word I said to Chris in frustration with this disease.

And, ummm... Let's not forget, I'm the one with the daunting task of picking up all these broken pieces and doing damage control with my kids. With *Chris's* kids. What I need is support.

Not a day goes by that I don't think about Chris's death for one reason or another. A person who lives with an alcoholic for ten years is bound to have recurring thoughts, and the memories seem to hit at the strangest times. It festers enough on its own without this blame game.

I simply refuse to sit in silence, seething in this sickening and twisted attempt at condemnation. What these blamers and shamers don't know about me is that I don't sit quietly anymore when I'm wronged. I have a voice, a loud one, and I no longer make concessions in my life. Except nachos. I love those concessions.

I can't know that something atrocious like this happens without doing something about it. I cannot take the chance that anyone else, that you dear reader, might someday experience this type of mistreatment. Or, that you may be made to feel at fault for something you had absolutely no control over.

And I'm not just talking about the death of a loved one with alcoholism. Not all alcoholics die, but they still wreak havoc on the lives of the people nearest to them - and difficult decisions have to be made.

To anyone reading this who is struggling with their self worth like I once was, please imagine me gently holding your hands in mine, as I look into your eyes and speak directly into your heart: It's more than okay to protect yourself - even when others don't agree with you. You are not selfish. This isn't your fault.

Here's a little reminder for us all:

"Alcoholism isn't caused by our family problems, our actions, our inactions, what we've said or haven't said, or how we appear. Alcoholics might blame their drinking on the people they love, but they drink because they have a disease. It's as simple as that."

— HOW AL-ANON WORKS

Hide behind the kids' needs if you must, but you are allowed to do what's best for you as well. And you should.

After trying to change and control my husband's alcoholism for ten entire years, I was so miserable that I wanted to die.

That type of anguish isn't something that anyone can understand unless they've been through it themselves. So, yeah. I had to protect myself, and you have every right to do the same, if that's what you choose to do.

Newsflash to the unhealed shamers, blamers, and guilt projectors out there: That! Isn't! Selfish! Extra, extra! Read all about it!

30

HARD TRUTH

STOP SEEKING VALIDATION FROM OTHERS.

Dear readers, why in the world are we allowing others to force their twisted ideas onto us of how this one life we get should be lived? Why do we seek authorization and permission from others to do what we want and need? Who are we allowing to trick us into thinking that we ever mattered less than everyone else?

Are you finding yourself in a similar situation, friends? Repeat after me: Not today, Satan.

I mean, honestly? It makes zero sense for anyone to care for themselves last. And yet that's our first response in crisis. Even if you're not yet ready to make any drastic changes to your situation, it's at least something to chew on for a bit.

There's a reason why flight attendants ask us to put our own oxygen masks on first before helping others when an airplane is in distress.

Wanna know why in my words? Well, ready or not, I'm going to tell you... Because we fucking matter too. That's why.

I could sit here and give tiptoe answers that we hear all the time like, "If we don't take care of ourselves first, we can't take care of others."

Okay, yeah. Sure. We are caretakers and that makes sense. Buuuut... it's a crock of shit. ~~The real answer,~~ No, the only answer to why it's okay to protect ourselves is: We matter. I matter, and you matter. Our wants and needs matter. And we get to decide what's best for us. Period.

That doesn't mean that we don't have empathy for others, or that we don't care for others well enough. It doesn't mean that we suck as mothers or as wives, and it sure as hell doesn't mean that we are selfish.

It means that we fucking matter.

31

MY SECOND DIVORCE

As I started to find my self-worth, I began fighting an internal battle of what was worse - Chris staying at home and things continuing to be out of control, or Chris leaving and taking his drama with him.

There had been a lot of knock down, drag out fighting in the few weeks prior to Chris moving out; really in the last year or so of our marriage. Both of our boys were greatly affected by it each and every time.

Chris spent the entire week prior to leaving in a tumultuous detox - drinking binge - detox cycle and I found myself feeling that 'knowing' I mentioned before. My gut, my heart, and my mind were finally aligned and in full agreement. I knew it was time. Chris had to move out.

Our youngest son was turning into a sort-of middleman during our fights, reminding us of all the good times we had in the past as a family. He'd say things like, "Do you remember when we all used to build Legos in my room on the floor? Can we go build Legos today?" The way his tiny voice trembled in fear and panic while he did this was enough to stop my heart completely, you guys.

Bless his little heart for thinking things were that easy to fix. And shame on me and Chris for putting him through that.

Our oldest son started becoming my little protector and replacement partner. I cannot, no matter how hard I try, get the image of my eleven year old defending me with his pre-pubescent voice yelling, "Don't talk to my mom that way!" Or, "It's okay, Mom, I'll help you," as he'd place his small hand on top of mine. No child should ever feel the need to protect one parent while becoming a substitution for the other.

If I had to pick out my most painful memories from our experience with this disease, these would certainly be two of them. The lump in my throat always shows up when I think about it.

Slow, deep breaths, y'all. This is extremely tough stuff. It was all really, really heartbreaking for me to watch at the time and is even more difficult to write about almost two years later.

Tears are literally streaming down my face as I choose the right words to document these heartbreaking memories with.

It was at this point in time that I knew, in the depths of my soul, that Chris had very little choice left on whether or not he drank. This disease had a firm grip on him, and had already begun taking its toll. He didn't want *this* for our kids with as much conviction as I didn't want it for them, but he couldn't stop.

We were able to sit the kids down as a parenting team and explain to the boys that Daddy needed to go live with Grandpa for a little while. We omitted details on why, in order to preserve what innocence they had left, but they very much knew that Daddy was sick. So naturally, we took the, "He's going to live there so we don't fight anymore while he's trying to get better" approach.

When Chris left, he went quietly. He wasn't happy about it, being especially vocal about what little space his dad's house had for him. But he, too, understood that it was time. He left on good-ish terms; all four of us were crying and in utter agony, but he was calm.

My heart physically hurt watching Chris pack up his stuff and leave, you guys. It felt as if it were going to either explode or break into pieces - a literal broken heart. I was sad, but I wasn't grieving for myself. I was grieving for Chris and for our children.

I knew this was the right thing or I wouldn't have done it. I was doing the hard thing because it was what needed to be done. No more waiting to see what was going to happen.

Needless to say, emotions were high, but we decided together before he left that he could (and should) come home often to visit the kids. We both wanted him to continue to be involved in the boys' lives while he tried to get better. Plans were made for him to visit the next day and he did.

I was hoping that, like the first go-round of craziness five years earlier, Chris would hit rock bottom and realize what he lost - our family. I knew we were nearing the end of our time as a family of four.

This was our Hail Mary.

Asking Chris to leave our home, in no way, defines the way any of us felt about him. Besides burying him, asking him to leave was the hardest thing I've ever had to do. I knew how much he was struggling.

This was my choice to make, and I made it.

As terrible and complicated as it is, this is simply an effect of the disease of alcoholism. None of us wanted Chris gone, none of us wanted this for our family; we all just absolutely needed the craziness to fucking stop.

Halloween 2019 rolled around just four days after Chris moved out. It was the scariest Halloween I've ever had. See what I did there? All joking aside, witches, goblins, and ghosts got nothin' on alcoholism. The kids were missing their dad a lot (we all were), so he came over to Trick-or-Treat with us.

When he arrived, he was very clearly not feeling well. We walked our small town together for a few hours and when the kids ran up to the different houses to get candy, I had a few opportunities to chat with him privately.

He was mostly quiet and withdrawn, but when I asked him if he was feeling okay and he assured me he was fine. He couldn't hide his sickness from me that day no matter how hard he tried; I had seen him detox too many times.

Chris had a kind heart and this time I knew he was lying to protect me. It didn't work. I wonder sometimes if his compulsive lying for all those years was him trying to shield me from pain. I don't know why asking him if he felt well was even a thing I decided to do because the answer was obvious.

32

THE SPIRAL

Detox is the common term used by most people when referring to Alcohol Withdrawal Syndrome. According to americanaddictioncenters.org, When a person with significant alcohol dependence suddenly stops drinking, the brain and nervous system may become temporarily hyperexcitable, potentially giving rise to these things:

- Anxiety
- Agitation
- Insomnia
- Irritability

- Upset stomach, nausea, vomiting
- Tremors (the shakes)
- Seizures

www.americanaddictioncenters.org

At times, a person might develop more severe symptoms, such as high fevers, hallucinations, grand mal seizures, and severe mental confusion.

Severe and/or complicated alcohol withdrawal can be life threatening, and may require close medical monitoring for symptom development in addition to the use of certain sedating medications (e.g. benzodiazepines) to minimize seizure risks during the withdrawal period.

Medical detox can help keep an alcohol dependent patient as safe and comfortable as possible during withdrawal... The more [a person] drink[s], the more likely [they] are to experience alcohol withdrawal.

Other factors that may influence the [type] and severity of alcohol withdrawal include the following:

- An underlying medical or psychiatric condition
- How long [the person has] been abusing alcohol
- How much [the person] drinks
- How recently [the person] last used alcohol

- Whether [the person has] previously experienced withdrawal complications such as seizures.

americanaddictioncenters.org

If you remember from earlier in my memoir, Chris had a seizure seven years before his death. This means that his alcoholism was in the severe stages, even back then. I was this many years old when I learned this while researching for my memoir.

That Halloween, Chris's hands were shaking so badly (tremors), that he was unable to unwrap Trick-or-Treat candy wrappers for the boys when they asked him to. Their tiny hands had gloves on.

I decided that it was time for the lying to stop so I simply told him, very calmly, that I knew what was happening to him; he was in detox again. By now I could tell what was going on even if it wasn't spoken out loud.

He gave me a nod, but it was obvious he didn't want to talk about anything related to the situation, so just asked him to try to take care of his basic needs... You know, drinking water, eating meals and sleeping at night. And, I told him that I was there for him to help in any way even though he wasn't living at the house anymore. He didn't respond, but it was important for me to at least let him know out loud.

33

DETOX AND REHAB

B y early November 2019, Chris was still struggling. He'd
come to the house a few times a week to visit the kids
and each time it was clear how extremely sick he was. One
evening, I was fearful that he would get in a car accident due to
his extreme tremors and just overall appearance of fatigue. So, I
had him sleep in the basement.

The next day was Veteran's Day, so the kids and I were
home from school. Around 10 o'clock that morning, I
thought it was odd that Chris hadn't come upstairs at all, so
went down to see him lying face first, seizing into the
couch.

Once he regained consciousness, we sat together and cried. We
were both very scared - as an extreme understatement. This was
the very first time Chris accepted my suggestion for

professional help, and admitted himself into a local detox facility that day.

The very last time I sat with Chris one-on-one was during our allotted one hour visitation window while he was in a local detox facility. I came to bring him a few things, as he was preparing to leave for Chicago in a few days for rehab.

I have to say, this was one of my most favorite memories with Chris of all time. I know, I know, he was in a detox facility and heading to rehab. But, he was so healthy and light hearted and positive... I had not seen him that well in years. I saw the Chris I knew and loved, he had a very lively sparkle in his eye.

We laughed as I showed him how to fill in a Sudoku puzzle, we had a really good, really deep conversation, he told me how badly he wanted things to change.

It was the last time I ever hugged Chris, and the last time we spoke the words, "I love you." I told him how proud of him I was, he gave me a letter for the kids... and that was that.

Chris's last Thanksgiving alive was in November of 2019, and he spent it in Chicago's Haymarket Rehabilitation Center. It wasn't a very happy Thanksgiving for our family; that empty chair at the table was gut wrenching to see.

Chris called us to say Happy Thanksgiving, but I unfortunately missed the call and wasn't allowed to call back. He didn't leave a message.

He returned home from rehab two days before Christmas, and was found at the liquor store less than a week later. He may as well have gotten out a knife and stabbed me directly into my heart. This was the final blow.

34

HARD TRUTH - THE SEQUEL:
IF YOU CONTINUE TO ENABLE THE ADDICT,
YOU'LL EVENTUALLY BURY HIM.

C hris continued to visit the kids while trying to stay sober after rehab. In my true enabling ways, what allowing Chris to come back to visit so freely did, in reality, was give him the best of both worlds. He was free to drink and do what he wanted while away from home, and he still got to see the kids every day.

Sigh.

Though there is a lot of guilt that comes with that, as a recovering spouse of an alcoholic I now know this: I could not control his drinking no matter where he was living.

It is easy to say I should have done this, or I shouldn't have done that. Please hear me when I say this, friends. We can't take on someone else's sobriety. At the end of the day, his alcoholism was not my battle to fight. Likewise, your loved one's alcoholism is not your battle to fight.

I enabled Chris because I didn't know better at the time. Look, in all honesty, it was so freaking hard to see him go through this over and over again. I fought this disease with him side by side for so many years and that white flag I had to raise felt as heavy as a boulder.

My enabling, coupled with my inability to completely cut ties, was certainly part of the problem; however, it wasn't *the* problem. My intentions were good, but all it did was prevent Chris from feeling this loss in its entirety.

Hey, friends and fellow weary spouses, if you're having these same feelings, I know they're excruciatingly painful, and I want to take a moment to just acknowledge that. You're doing the best you can. I see you. My heart is with you.

Moving out of our family home was a pivotal moment in Chris's life. Detox and rehab was another one. If he didn't start going to frequent AA meetings and work the program diligently, he was not going to be able to free himself from the death grip this disease had on him.

I knew that at the time, but there was nothing I could do about it except pray and try to encourage him. My hope for him to get better was not going to be enough. He had to put the work in.

Sadly, Chris was never able to work the program. The pandemic hit during such a crucial time in his recovery and when the world shut down, Alcoholics Anonymous meetings and Al-Anon meetings turned to online formatting.

Chris refused to attend zoom meetings - no matter how many links I sent him.

Me via text on May 16th, 2020:
"You should join that zoom, Chris, it would make me feel better [for you to visit with the kids] if you were going to meetings. My sister said it's a good one."

Chris's response via text:
"I understand. I'm still getting things organized on my end though. My job, bills, all types of shit. Unemployment. I'm trying to get back on my feet. I'm broke. Living on nothing and stressed out. Zoom is the last thing I need right now. My priorities are working on me right now."

Me: *"Going to meetings is you working on yourself. Zoom is the first thing you need right now."*

Chris: *"Ok."*

Me: *"So, if you want to take the boys fishing tomorrow, please hit up a meeting before then. That's*

an important part of this and your response to it this
morning is scary to me."

(crickets)

As time went on, Chris stopped coming around and the calls and texts became very infrequent. Then, they were no longer made at all. He wasn't attending meetings and things continued to spiral out of control.

Though I'll never know for sure, I correleate his lack of communication with me and the kids directly to the amount of alcohol he was drinking.

When I reached out to Chris, he always answered, but was often angry and always checked out. This was an all too familiar giant red flag for me that he was not doing well. When the entire country went into lockdown, his alcoholism saw it's chance and escalated.

That being said, being the spouse of an active alcoholic was no longer going to work for me. And, well... It was time for me to formally turn in my resignation to his disease. To Whom It May Concern: I quit. I'm done. Effective immediately.

This disease was forcing me to choose between my children and my husband, whom I didn't even feel like I knew anymore. I was also being forced to choose between my husband and myself.

Knowing how much I was struggling was the final deciding factor. In addition to that, our kids deserved one of their parents to be strong enough to make this near impossible decision for them. This killer disease had started taking over their dad's brain and ability to recover. It was just a matter of time before it took his life too.

Deep down, I knew that this was not going to get better for me, so I decided to file for divorce. Chris and I talked extensively about our divorce and were in mutual agreement on the big things.

More than anything else in the world, I wanted him to get better, be the dad I knew he could be, and find peace and happiness in his own life. I was searching for peace and happiness myself as well.

Chris was allowed to see the kids whenever he wanted, per our divorce decree, with the stipulation that he was working an AA program and wasn't drinking. And, I waved all child support from him - in the present and future - because I very much wanted him to be able to get back on his feet and work with me as a parenting team.

DENIAL TURNED ACCUSATORY

J umping forward to the week before Chris passed away, I received a middle of the night phone call from one of his college buddies, who... I'll call Gio. Gio was calling to express his concerns about Chris and wanted to know what was going on.

I hadn't heard from Gio in years and it quickly became clear that he wasn't exactly 'in the loop'. I gave a general explanation of what was going on - and told him about our month old divorce. And, I let him know that I was worried about Chris as well but checking on him daily as best as I could.

Gio told me he had known about the divorce, as Chris had visited him for a weekend a few months prior. However, he was under the impression that our divorce was what was causing Chris's drinking problem.

Ummm.

Just no.

What in the actual fuck?

More lies from Chris.

When I asked Gio what sparked his worries about Chris, he explained that Chris's new long distance girlfriend, a mutual friend of theirs, had started to see some red flags. Good for her! Seriously.

Gio had also encountered his own odd situation during Chris's recent visit. He explained that he had left Chris alone at his place in order to drive his children back to their mom's house. When he returned, he noticed that next to his visibly emptier liquor bottles, lay a handful of his kids' empty Go-Gurt Squeeze wrappers.

He thought this was strange, so he went back to his surveillance videos in his living room (that he claimed were there because he had house cleaners and guns). He saw Chris chugging his booze directly from the bottles and chasing it with the yogurt.

Less than a week after that phone call, Chris died. His friends were understandably distraught. They became furious at me for 'abandoning him when he needed me the most' and 'not reaching out to them for help'.

One such friend... I'll call this one Cale, even proclaimed that he could have 'saved' Chris if he knew how bad things had gotten. Mmhmm... Cale clearly doesn't understand how alcoholism works, but there was no telling him that.

I was blamed for Chris's death multiple times by these 'friends' of his even though they experienced his alcoholic behaviors for themselves over the course of many years. I guess they never stopped to think that I might not have been able to continue to live with these same types of erratic behaviors... Or... You know wanted my kids to.

"I know I'm asking tough questions, but my friend is dead and there's this whole secret life that was going on that I just want to understand... I know it's tough right now but I'm just so confused. There are people in this world that can deal with reality and don't put up a facade that they have a perfect life, while behind closed doors all hell is breaking loose... I am very sickened."

— CALE

They were so 'sickened' by me (and, I'm guessing, themselves) that only one of Chris's many college friends attended his visitation or funeral. And... Hold onto your seats for this one, friends... That one college friend wasn't Gio or Cale. Gasp!

I've thought long and hard about how I want to approach this part of my story and whether or not I even want to approach it directly to these people at all.

My original thoughts are... Ummm... Excuse me, but can any and all blamers and shamers please get the eff out of my hula hoop and back into their own?

But ultimately, I've decided that it's not worth my time and energy to try to fight my corner this time. But, I will share my thoughts with you, my dear readers.

Hi, Chris's college friends. I know you're here lurking and I'm glad you've stopped by. Hopefully you've gotten some insight on how detrimental the disease of alcoholism has been on our entire family. Thank you for helping to inspire me to write this book.

My decision to not engage in this comes twofold. Chris shared half-truths with his college friends; actually more like one-eighth truths. Besides that, my feelings have always been and will always be valid.

First and foremost, I'm (still) not here to defend myself or my decisions and actions. If a person hasn't lived in my shoes (or yours), they could never understand our personal journey. I don't expect them to. I just also don't expect them to start pointing fingers, but here we are.

Second, it wouldn't do any good to hash this out with them anyway. They're firm in their beliefs and I'm too secure and healed from the calamity of this disease for anyone else to tell me otherwise. Seriously, healed people kinda think it's laughable when unhealed people try to tell them how they feel.

Look, truth be told, Chris's friends would have been in waaaay over their heads if they knew the full story. They couldn't have helped, even if they tried their hardest. Based on my experience with telling Chris's lifelong best friend, Chris wouldn't have allowed it.

If these college friends really knew Chris in this stage of his life, versus the college partying stage, they would have known how much he was struggling - without me having to tattle on him.

They'd also have known that Chris would never ever, in a million years, want them blaming me for what happened.

I am the only person on the planet that knows what ~~we~~ I went through; I'm the only person alive that knows the full truth. And I'm the only person that... Wait for it... Gets to make decisions for my own life.

When someone misplaces this type of blame, their ignorance is very elementary. I don't mean ignorance by way of name calling, I mean the literal definition of ignorance - a lack of knowledge or information.

You see, Chris didn't tell his friends what was happening in its entirety because he didn't want them to know.

Second, I didn't tell these particular friends because, well... I didn't *want* to tell them. It wasn't my place, and they weren't the right people to tell.

If they want to assume that I didn't reach out to anyone for help and tossed Chris to the side when I was done with him, then so be it. That nonsense is their own unhealthy coping mechanism that allows them to not feel guilty themselves.

Rest assured that everyone who needed to know, did.

Oh, and honestly, his friends *did* know. They already had their own experiences with Chris and his alcoholism. They had seen enough to know that there was an ongoing problem. It wasn't my responsibility to tell them when to check up on their friend. They chose not to reach out.

Here's their hard truth: Unhealthy people need someone to blame in difficult situations to cover up their own guilt and shame. I don't have much more to say about it except - it's not a nice thing to do to people.

My hope for them is that they find a way to heal their own difficult feelings in a healthier way. Blaming me doesn't, and never will, make it go away.

Dear readers, if you, too, have anyone judging the difficult decisions you've been forced to make because of someone else's battle with alcoholism I'd like you to read the following quote over and over again until it sinks all the way in.

I give you Theodore Roosevelt:

"It is not the critic who counts; not the man who points out how the strong man stumbles, or where the doer of deeds could have done them better. The credit belongs to the man who is actually in the arena, whose face is marred by dust and sweat and blood; who strives valiantly; who errs, who comes short again and again, because there is no effort without error and shortcoming; but who does actually strive to do the deeds; who knows great enthusiasms, the great devotions; who spends himself in a worthy cause; who at the best knows in the end the triumph of high achievement, and who at the worst, if he fails, at least fails while daring greatly, so that his place shall never be with those cold and timid souls who neither know victory nor defeat."

— THEODORE ROOSEVELT, 1910

"If you are not in the arena also getting your ass kicked, I am not interested in your feedback."

— DR. BRENE BROWN

VII

LET HIM REST IN PEACE

There are moments that change your life forever. At any time, something can happen that makes you realize that nothing will ever be the same. These moments divide time into a 'before this' and an 'after this'.

— ANONYMOUS

Chris was pronounced dead by the coroner at 8:38 am on July 2, 2020, just one month before his 38th birthday. Strangely enough, that was the exact same minute that I sent a text to his father asking if he was okay.

I somehow subconsciously knew the very moment his death became official.

The day before Chris passed away, I contacted him, worried, because I knew he hadn't been doing well. I called and he didn't answer. So, I sent a text: "Are you doing ok? I called to check in and you didn't answer." He responded with, "I'm not feeling well." That was the very last text he ever sent me.

I immediately called him and he picked up. I could hear how ill he was and knew that he was in the middle of a harsh detox. By then, I could hear the sound of detox in Chris's voice. To anyone else, it would sound like someone who had the flu. He was shivering and having trouble speaking because he was weak and out of breath.

Detox from alcohol is the most dangerous type of detox there is. Though detoxing from all addictive substances is painful and causes a person to become ill, detoxing from alcohol is the only one that can actually kill a person.

I learned this from the nurses that were caring for Chris the last time he was in a detox facility. Because I knew he was in danger again, I begged him to let me come get him and take him to a hospital. He refused.

His final spoken words to me were forced through chattering teeth. He wheezed, "I'll be fine, [Annie], I just need to lay down."

He wasn't fine.

Scrambling for any help I could get, I hung up with Chris and then called his dad, whom he lived with at the time, and told him how dire it was that Chris was brought to a hospital right away.

I don't know what happened after that other than Chris didn't get to the hospital and instead was found dead in his bedroom the next morning.

In retrospect, I wish I would have just gone over there myself and forced him to go. I knew how sick he was from interactions I had with him the week before he died. And, I knew how dangerous detox was.

Here's the deal - and this is the hard, honest truth - by this time I wasn't Chris's wife anymore. I was working hard to stop trying to control everything. So, I didn't force him to go.

And, I have to live with that guilt every day for the rest of my life. Or, until I learn how to forgive myself for it. The healed parts of me know that it wouldn't have mattered in the end. It would have possibly prolonged the inevitable. But, I still wish I would have taken him myself.

There were so many people in this man's life that loved him, and his life ended, tragically, with only his dog by his side. The image of him laying there still haunts me every single day of my life and I didn't even see him the morning he passed away.

More deep breaths.

The paramedics dragged Chris's naked body out of his dad's house wrapped in bedsheets because it was too hoarded to fit a stretcher inside.

I don't know why he was naked, but I can painfully guess that he was either extremely hot or hallucinating. It was a horrific scene straight out of anyone's worst nightmares... And I can't shake it from my brain. I didn't need to be there to witness it for myself; the details I was given were enough to create my own visual image. It's so fucking heart breaking how all of this went down.

This is alcoholism, sweet friends. This is what this terrible disease does to people's husbands. To little kids' fathers. To people's brothers. To people's best friends. To people's children. To people with a Master's Degree and a family that loves them.

36

HARD TRUTH

PEOPLE REALLY DO DIE FROM ALCOHOLISM.

The CDC uses the term 'excessive alcohol use' when referring to alcohol related deaths. The shocking reality is that an average of 261 people die from excessive alcohol use daily in the United States.

Two hundred sixty one.

I'll let that one sink in a moment...

That adds up to about 95,000 people annually. People who are loved and who have families and children who need them. Die. Every day. Because of alcoholism.

I'm not trying to scare anyone here, but I was one of those people that used to think, "That will never happen to us."

I guess I should be clear and say Chris wasn't my husband when he died. Not anymore. He died just 45 days after our divorce was finalized. I'm learning that when telling the story of a loved one who lost their life so horribly, labels tend to disappear.

Our divorce was so new and we had so many secrets that even people in our inner circle didn't know we were living apart, let alone no longer married. I planned and paid for his visitation and funeral, as his wife, out of nothing but love for him and devastation of the loss of him.

Maybe I couldn't be married to him anymore; maybe I had been through too much to keep living that kind of rollercoaster life... The day in and day out ups and downs and spins and spirals were making me sick too, and I found myself wondering when the eff this ride was finally going to end so I could get off.

That doesn't negate the fact that I cared deeply for this man, and he died. Husband, ex husband, who cares? This disease forced him to leave me and our marriage behind years ago, as well as our young children who were merely nine and twelve years old when alcoholism took his life.

37

THE HIDDEN GIFT OF DIVORCE

Our divorce was a very important piece of this puzzle as it did a few things for both of us, before he died, that allowed for an enormous gift called forgiveness.

The last time I saw Chris alive was just a week before he passed away. I met him at his childhood home to go over a few things that would finalize the refinancing of our marital home. I needed a signature from him.

We were supposed to meet at the bank, but he told me he wasn't feeling well enough to make it there. Angrily, I went to him. But, when I got to his house, I was in absolute shock at what I saw. I had seen this man sick countless times in our marriage because of this disease, but I had never seen him like *this*. He was standing, holding onto the railing of the porch, swaying back and forth.

I knew what was happening. He was drunk. But not because he wanted to be. He needed to be. For some reason, this time, instead of belittling him and asking him to 'get better for his kids', I sat on the step and asked him to join me.

His hands were shaking so badly he couldn't even sign the check. A sure sign of detox. I know I just said that he was drunk, because he was. But, after living with him for ten years, I knew his behaviors well. He was drinking to stop the painful and very dangerous side effects of detox.

We sat silently for a few moments as I gathered up enough courage to ask if he was okay. You see, I knew that this had become so much more than just another detox or another relapse. His skin was yellow. He was trembling all over. And, his stomach, ankles, and feet were swollen.

Chris broke the silence by saying, "I'm not doing well, [Annie]".

He went on to say how hard not being at home with his family had been on him. As I sit here and write this, I'm reminded once again why I sometimes feel like I, in fact, did kill Chris. Even though, in the depths of my soul and in every single ounce of my being, I know that there was nothing more I could have done for him.

It was then that I took off his favorite hat, his fitted St. Louis Cardinals hat. Much to my surprise, his hair was grown out and dyed blonde. He had on an old pair of broken glasses, and I took those off too, so I could look directly into his bright blue eyes.

Tears were streaming from both my eyes and from his. I told him how loved he was and that his sons needed him to be strong and to find a way to beat this disease. I told him that I was always going to be there for him. And that the next day I'd be back to take him for lunch, a haircut, and to order some new glasses for him.

He replied by telling me he was too sick to go anywhere, and I promised I would at least call to see if he was feeling better.

I then ended this moment by sobbing, "Don't make me bury you."

Looking back on it now, I better understand why he stopped contacting the boys and I. ~~He didn't live with us any longer... But he could have at least called to see if we were okay or if we needed anything.~~ He was too sick to. That's something I couldn't see clearly at the time and I carry a lot of guilt around with me about how angry I was with him.

38

HARD TRUTH

THE ALCOHOLIC IS SUFFERING TOO.

This next hard truth is a tough one, friends. When we're going through all the really chaotic and heartbreaking parts of our spouse's alcoholism, it's really easy to focus on our own pain and anger. Alternatively, it's really difficult to stop and have empathy for the alcoholic.

I don't know about your loved one who is struggling, but I do know this about mine: He was no longer himself when the alcohol stole the last breath from his lungs. Alcoholism took Chris's mind well before it took his body. It changed who he was and how he acted.

The most important thing our divorce did for me was releasing me as Chris's victim and giving me the freedom to start having empathy and compassion for him. I went from his victim to his biggest cheerleader, snap, just like that.

My readings about this have taught me to see Chris, not as an alcoholic, but as a person with alcoholism. I've learned that when I was able to see the disease of alcoholism as the cause of his behaviors I could detach from the victimization of all of it.

This is a great reminder for us all that the alcoholic is suffering too; every single human on this planet is worthy of love, even those who we feel are harming us.

"Resentment will do nothing except tear us apart inside. No one ever found serenity through hatred. No one ever truly recovered from the effects of alcoholism by harboring anger or fear, or by holding on to grudges. Hostility keeps us tied to the abuses of the past. Even if the alcoholic is long gone from our lives or has refrained from drinking for many years, we, too, need to learn to detach. We need to step back from the memories of alcoholic behavior that continue to haunt us... We too, must find within us compassion for the alcoholic who suffered from this terrible illness."

— HOW AL-ANON WORKS

The funeral home graciously offered to type up Chris's obituary, but I felt compelled to write it for him. I wanted to capture who Chris really was, and not focus on what had become of him.

Chris was a goofball, the life of the party. His obituary needed to match his personality. I was honored to write it for him and thought of it as one last gift from me to him.

Besides this memoir, Chris's obituary was both the easiest and most difficult thing I have ever written. As I sat behind my computer screen that hot summer day, I was flooded with memories and the good times we all shared as a family.

It was this very moment I realized that through the process of our divorce, I grieved the loss of our marriage and family unit. And, through his death I was mourning this loss of my dear friend and all of the unfinished things we were supposed to experience together in this life.

Things like watching our sons earn their diplomas, walk down the aisles at their weddings, and celebrating the birth of our grandchildren.

Talk about pain.

Deepest breaths ever.

Friends, this is the gut wrenching reality of alcoholism. It kills people. It leaves families in ruin. It brings ex wives to the table, bawling, wondering how she's ever going to come back from this, how she will ever get her children to feel okay again.

It wasn't until after Chris died that I realized I, too, acted like an alcoholic at times. Irrational. Angry. Out of control. Lost. When this sort of thing happens to you, you feel crazy disoriented all.the.time.

I found myself irate with Chris more often than not for 'not getting better for us/the kids/me/our family.' I was disappointed in him and he knew it.

So much guilt.

Looking back at it, I now know that I was grieving the loss of the family I planned for myself and just doing the best I could with what I knew at the time.

I often joke around about Al-Anon or any other twelve step program being a prerequisite to marriage. I often wonder if I knew then what I know now... Would Chris still be alive? It's impossible to know. But, my honest to goodness guess is that he would not be. He needed to work his own program for his life to be saved.

39

OBITUARY

C hristopher, age 37, died at his childhood home on Thursday, July 2, 2020. He attended Western Illinois University, where he earned his Bachelor's and Master's Degrees in Information Technology. It took him a few years longer than most to earn them, but his dad will say that's only because he was having too much fun living the college life.

Chris was a talented computer specialist and was responsible for creating and maintaining IT programs at various businesses in the area. He most enjoyed building servers and working with dear friends downtown, then walking down the street to Busch Stadium to watch the Cardinals dominate the Cubs.

The more meaningful things in Chris's life were centered on spending time with the people who loved him, especially his boys. His son and his step-son whom he loved and raised as his own, were the focus of Chris's energy and time.

He was happiest with his boys, took them fishing often, and eagerly watched their soccer games, basketball games, and guitar and drum lessons. He had the loudest, laugh-y cheer of all the parents in the crowd when the boys scored a goal.

If you've ever seen Chris excited, then you're hearing his outrageous laugh right now. There's no doubt that Chris's laugh was contagious and unforgettable.

[His youngest son] gained his love of basketball from his dad, and the two could recite the best players of every team throughout basketball history like champs. [His son] proudly displays a Michael Jordan, Kobe Bryant, and LeBron James poster in his room that his dad surprised him with for doing well in school.

Chris and [his youngest son] also shared a love for bobble heads, which Chris purchased for him on special occasions. You'll find their favorite, Reaper, displayed at Chris's memorial visitation.

Chris was a scary movie connoisseur, an avid Cardinals and Blues fan, and spent countless hours playing on the floor with the boys, pretending to be Batman and Superman. If [his youngest son] could spend one more day with his dad, this is what he would choose to do. Chris had his Batman voice down pat and we hope he always knew that he was [our oldest son] and [our youngest son]'s real life superhero.

Chris loved to play video games with his children and friends who are scattered throughout the United States. Every Friday night you could catch Chris having a 'boys only' sleepover in the basement with his sons, frat house style. These precious times hold [his step-son's] favorite memories with him.

[Their] last great memory of [their] dad was playing Fortnite online with him, a game that Chris hated, but loved to play with his pride and joy. He had strong convictions about the ideals he was passionate about and probably should have been a lawyer because he had a quick and witty counter argument for everything.

His love for rap music became hilarious when the boys learned all the lyrics to Run-D.M.C.'s 'It's Tricky'.

There is no doubt that Chris loved his family and friends. But above all, he loved his weird looking and overly bark-y dachshund, Skeeter, who annoyed everyone on the planet except for Chris. Please say a small prayer for this little dog, as he is surely missing his best friend today.

There was so much good in Chris; he was friendly and fun, always the life of the party, had a heart of gold, and gave the best cuddles to the boys when they were sick, sorry Mom. He will be painfully missed.

Chris battled through some tough struggles in his life and fought bravely for as long as he could. In the words of Jack Burton from Chris's favorite movie, Big Trouble in Little China, "I'm a reasonable guy, but I've just experienced some very unreasonable things."

He was preceded in death by his mother, who died in 1989. Surviving are his father, his brother, his son, his step-son, his grandmother, his former wife and dear friend, [Annie], and his crazy dog Skeeter.

VIII

MY SAVING GRACE

"Love, it will not betray you, dismay, or enslave you.

It will set you free.

Be more like the man you were made to be.

There is a design, an alignment,

a cry of my heart to see the beauty of love

as it was made to be."

— MUMFORD AND SONS, SIGH NO MORE

In this section of my story, I'm gonna flip the script and start transitioning our hard truths into softer ones. It's time for us to start believing that we deserve better from this life, friends; alcoholism doesn't have to be a death sentence.

Something profound that I've learned as I'm finding my way is that when I'm trying too hard to accomplish something, forcing it if you will, things generally work out better for me. I just have to redirect my energy and try softer instead.

Life doesn't have to always be so hard, friends. It really doesn't. Whatever you want your life to be like and feel like - is always within your reach. If you're still struggling to give yourself permission to live your best life, I see you. I feel you. I *was* you. I still am you sometimes.

The hurt that this disease causes cuts deep, like to the bone. And I'm not sure if it's something that can ever be completely healed. Or even should be completely healed for that matter.

What I do know is that scars don't hurt like open wounds do. I hope that my story has shown you that you're not alone with your struggles. And even if it's just in a small way, I hope I've been able to give you an iota of inspiration to start loving yourself unconditionally.

40

SOFT TRUTH

YOU HAVE THE POWER TO TURN DOUBT
AND UNCERTAINTY INTO HOPE.

L ife is always evolving and changing its course. For the first time in... Oh... The history of ever, I'm really excited to see what comes next for me. I'm so very ready to be me, unapologetically, and trust that everything else will fall into place.

I'd like to end this part of my story by leaving you with a really beautiful explanation of how to find hope in what may seem to be the most hopeless of times.

Over the years, I've started meditating in an attempt to calm my mind and soul.

My favorite meditations are done with Deepak Chopra, meditation guru and advocate for alternative medicine, and Oprah Winfrey, no introduction needed for this inspirational lady.

Together, they're very insightful, and a few times a year they offer free 21 day meditations on their mobile app. Free and insightful are both right up my alley.

One of their meditations has really impacted my vision on turning doubt and uncertainty into hope and I simply cannot end this book without sharing it with you first. These are my paraphrased notes from that mediation:

Follow your dreams. The world is unfolding exactly as it's supposed to... In your favor.

When it feels like nothing is going your way or it seems like your path is being blocked by outside forces in your relationships, think about your typical reaction.

Do you move toward feelings of resentment or do you pause and ask, "What is my life trying to tell me right now?"

How you respond to the different things that happen to you can mean the difference between living a life of anger or joy... Between despair and hope.

Eckhart Tolle, spiritual teacher and world renowned author, describes it like this: Life is an adventure, not a package tour. Being at ease with not knowing is crucial for answers to come to you. If you're dissatisfied in the unsettled state, you can't hear the guiding messages from your higher self.

Uncertainty is really your spirit's way of saying, "I'm in flux, something is off balance here."

Hope lives in these uncomfortable moments where you have doubts and don't know what to do. Well, when you don't know what to do... Get still. Wait for a guiding message from your higher self. That's where hope is. It rises up to meet you if you clear space and allow it.

On the journey of hope, fear can hold us back. Especially in uncertain times. Forces out there feel beyond our control.

By itself, uncertainty is neutral. Great things can come from it. Like the next important discovery, insight, or realization. Everything depends on how we choose to relate to uncertainty... Which is just life's constant stream of new events and challenges.

Becoming a source of hope, strength, and optimism allows you to embrace uncertainty. Without this inner strength of hope, we are left to suffer through crisis and uncertain times. With self doubt and fear, you feel weak and afraid.

When you doubt yourself, you can't trust anyone or anything. Everything reflects your inner doubt. You fear being let down, which is the same as expecting to be let down.

People who have been wounded and have lost hope may feel like life isn't fair. This means you have already surrendered your heart to the thing out there that defeated your hopes.

These things make dreams come true: Taking responsibility for your destiny, embracing the possibilities that arise today, being open and alert to changing situations, having a confident and flexible response to change, and finding solutions with obstacles and problems that block the way.

These are 'awareness skills' and it's totally realistic for you to develop them if you have hope.

— DEEPAK CHOPRA AND OPRAH
WINFREY

Just over a year ago, I was completely hopeless and pretty much sinking into a depression that could very well have taken my life. Now, I'm thriving and writing this memoir.

Back then, surrendering to 'what was' felt impossible and even laughable at times. Now, here I am filled with so much hope and love for myself, plowing through the hard times like a champ.

Reaching your personal life goals and watching your dreams come true is so opposite of impossible, beloved readers. All you have to do is accept life on life's terms and believe in yourself. Uncertainty is the only certainty we have in this life.

I know what you're probably thinking... That's easier said than done right? I guess that depends on how deep the desire is for change. There's only so much a person can endure before they reach their breaking point.

41

SOFT TRUTH

YOU ARE WORTHY OF A BETTER LIFE.

S weet reader, everything you've been through was not some sort of punishment or proclamation that you're unworthy of living a life that feels good. You aren't defective. In fact, you're the opposite of defective; you're a brave and capable work in progress.

Our hardships are wonderful teachers. Whether we like it or not, they give us the tools we need to move forward from everything that no longer fits.

Growing out of old versions of ourselves is no different than growing out of an old pair of jeans. We loved those jeans so much, right? They were comfortable and safe, and they hid all of our imperfections. Those jeans were our go-tos when we didn't know what else to wear, and we made so many memories in them.

They fit perfectly for a long, long time... But lately they just feel different. Those old jeans are feeling frumpy and looking outdated. And besides they're no longer in style anyway. Plus, they have that one stain and that hole in the back pocket that threatens to show our period panties whenever we wear them. You all know what I'm talking about.

These old jeans are just no longer going to work for us anymore. It's time to Marie Kondo that shit, Girl. Repeat after me: Goodbye old ~~jeans~~ me, thank you for everything you carried me through, you've done well. We made it all the way here together, but it's time for me to separate from my old self including habits and insecurities that are no longer appropriate to wear.

Whether or not your loved one is still actively drinking, and whether or not they're even playing an active role in your life... Ummm... Doesn't matter, dear one holding this book. Their drinking was never about you.

Your ability to walk forward toward your own personal hopes and dreams has been well earned. You've put in the time and energy! Now it's time for that raise you've been requesting through your prayers and manifesting with the universe.

At long last you can start to enjoy the rewards of living a life in turmoil.

Wait. Rewards from living a life in turmoil?

I said what I said... And I mean it too.

This disease doesn't just bring chaos. It brings wisdom and understanding, a deeper sense of gratitude for all the things that are good in our lives, compassion for others who are also struggling, a burning desire for more out of this life, and a big ass vault of strength gathered over the years that we're ready to unlock.

Let's move the fuck forward towards happiness, shall we?

42

SOFT TRUTH

THERE IS HELP AVAILABLE TO YOU IF YOU'RE LOOKING.

In January of 2020, just a few months after Chris left our home - before he died, I was a trainwreck again. I found my mind starting to wander once more to suicidal thoughts. I felt like I was drowning again, and it was debilitating me with an intensity I had not experienced before.

All of the effects of Chris's alcoholism had come to a head and ruptured in a disgusting mess all over my family's lives.

My therapist suggested I start attending Al-Anon meetings in addition to seeing her. My initial gut reaction was, 'Why'? I was making good progress in therapy, or so I wanted to think.

Plus, I was a super busy single mom working two jobs, going to therapy, taking the kids to therapy, and not sleeping at night. Then, there was homework, soccer practices and games for both boys, drum lessons for one kid and guitar lessons for the other. When the heck was I going to find the time to attend these meetings?

You guys, I was in so much freaking pain at this point. This was probably my personal lowest of lows. I was a mechanized, robot zombie floundering aimlessly, constantly trying to muster up enough strength just to function. I forced myself to check off the next thing on the to do list each morning.

I'd think, "Annie, you *have* to get out of bed. The kids need you to get out of bed. This isn't a choice." I had a mental checklist for myself:

☑ Take a shower, cry your feelings all the way out until you're numb

☑ Put your contacts in, seeing is a necessity

☑ Brush your teeth and get dressed

☑ Makeup? Eh...

☑ Wake the kids, feed the kids, hug and kiss the kids, pretend you're fine

☑ Eat something, you HAVE to eat something

☑ Get to school / work, there is a mountain of bills to pay

☑ Robot - Don't cry, be happy, smile... Actress mode activated

I was desperate for anything that might help me stop enduring such a miserable existence and allow me to start actually living my life. So, I wearily decided to give Al-Anon the old college try.

I questioned whether or not it could really help me *that* much? Was I a little skeptical? Sure, who wouldn't be? But, I very badly needed this program to work, and the only way to find out was to actually attend a meeting (or 6 - my Al-Anon buddies can get a good chuckle out of that one). I held onto hope because I was very quickly plummeting to my very own rock bottom.

I chose a Sunday morning meeting in a location near Target so I could swing by there and get groceries on the way home, feeding two birds with one scone (we don't kill birds with stones in our house).

My sons, who were only 8 and 11 years old at the time, had not yet ever stayed home without adult supervision. I fretted over leaving them alone because of this ugly thing called mom guilt. Plus, legally they weren't even allowed to be home alone.

I agonized over it, obsessively weighing my options. Back and forth I went until I finally decided that my oldest son was responsible enough to handle it and hold down the fort for two and a half hours, once a week. That's exactly how long it would take me to drive there, go to the meeting, run by Target for any necessities if I needed to, then drive home.

He had a cell phone that he could call or text me with whenever he wanted or needed, and we had an emergency plan for them to run to the neighbor's house together if they needed help quickly. Doors locked. Prayers said. Fingers crossed. Breathe in. Breathe out.

I'm, in no way, promoting anyone leaving their underaged children home alone to go to Al-Anon meetings, or to do anything else they need to do for that matter. I'm merely shining light on just how desperate I was to change my life.

We are each in a unique situation where we have to make our own decisions. The only insight I have for you on this is to do what you feel is best for all involved, including yourself, and adjust when needed.

I prepped the boys well for the time they'd be without me, bubble wrapping them as much as I could and practicing over and over again: Don't open the door for anyone, don't cook or eat any more food until I get back, don't fight, don't horse around, call or text me if you need anything at all... The list went on.

My protective Mama Bear Instinct was fierce as I attempted to shield them from more possible harm. It just so happens that the biggest harm I was trying to protect them from was all of the stupidity that this disease brought directly into our home.

Chris's alcoholism was haunting us and I sought healing for myself so I could proverbially sage it out... With love and light, get the fuck out of my house alcohol demons. Side note, I also literally tried to sage it out. I'm a tad witchy like that.

I no longer had a choice, friends. It was me and these two sweet boys against the world, and there was barely any 'me' left. I needed to do this for all three of us.

The meeting was held in a conference room in a hospital a few towns away from where we lived. I was really nervous and had no idea what to expect. I was so nervous, in fact, that I brought one of my closest friends with me for moral support.

Shout out! I love you, bessfran, thank you for always having my back.

In case you're curious about what these Al-Anon meetings are all about I'm going to describe my first meeting in depth. If you're not really interested in them yet, I promise not to dwell on it long; however, it can't hurt to at least hear my experience.

I walked in to about 15 smiling faces. Yes, I sure did say smiling faces - that wasn't a typo. How could that be? Weren't they at that meeting for the same reasons I was? I definitely wasn't smiling.

A few ladies popped up out of their seats with literal open arms to welcome me and tell me they were glad I was there.

These gentle humans didn't even know me or my story yet. They did; however, know that if I was there for the first time, I must have been dealing with some big, heavy stuff.

Immediately, I felt safe and welcome. There was an unspoken, sacred understanding between each of us that gave my heart and soul an instant sense of what I can only describe as relief and hope.

As I sat down and got my first chance to look around the room, I was kinda surprised at what I saw. The room was filled with people of mixed ages and races. I noticed that about one-third of the group was male, and I even saw two familiar faces.

The idea of seeing two familiar faces intimidated me at first, I'm not gonna lie. The gossip game in small towns is strong, friends. Since I live in the same small town I teach in, it's hard to find someone here who doesn't at least know who I am. I honestly had an 'Oh, shit' moment. I felt a little worried that I'd be outed or judged.

What I quickly realized was that these acquaintances were there for the same reason I was. And, I found that instead of feeling like they were judging me, I felt like we had a new and unique bond.

Anonymity is given utmost priority in Al-Anon meetings. They even state that during the meeting opening. Phew! This is how we feel safe enough to share in meetings.

I, ummm, may or may not have cried through my entire first meeting. Just kidding, I totally cried through my entire first meeting. And, still, nobody judged me. They just kept telling me they were glad that I was there. And they encouraged me to keep coming back, remembering a time that they, too, felt as trapped and as scared as I did.

Why did I cry so much you're wondering? That's simple. Because what my new friends were saying, in solidarity, hit me really hard:

"Clearly, a loved one's sobriety does not solve all our problems. Nor does physical separation, or even death. Even those of us who have not been involved with any alcoholics for many years find that we continue to be affected by the family disease. In short, the effects of alcoholism - obsession, anxiety, anger, denial, and feelings of guilt - tend to persist until we seek recovery for ourselves.

The problem is also within us. Al-Anon helps us to stop wasting time trying to change the things over which we have no control and to put our efforts to work where we do have some power - over our own lives."

— HOW ALANON WORKS

For the first time in what seemed like forever, I finally felt a spark of hope. I saw a glimpse of my light at the end of the very dark and twisted tunnel called alcoholism.

At the end of my first meeting I was asked to try six meetings before making a decision on whether or not this program was for me. They joked that if after six weeks I decide not to come back, they'd refund my misery.

Let's just say it didn't take me six weeks to realize how badly I needed to be supported by the Al-Anon community while I began to work on myself and heal.

Although Al-Anon has been both a literal and figurative life saver, it has only been a part of my saving grace. I promise to not ramble on and on about the program as this chapter of my story comes to a close.

Life is always ebbing and flowing. In fact, the only certainty in life is that it's bound to continuously change.

ENTERS, ERIC

Y ou see, Al-Anon is where I met my saving grace, the most amazing, patient, evolved, healthy, and wise human I've ever had the privilege to know. He's turned my life completely rightside up.

Eric and I met in January 2020 when I attended my very first Al-Anon meeting. The pandemic hit shortly after, and our Sunday 'Progress, Not Perfection' Al-Anon group resumed meetings via Zoom.

I was always in awe at the wisdom Eric shared in our meetings. He never seemed distressed; he was always calm and in control, and he used humor to share the revelations he gained along his own personal journey with this disease.

I find myself struggling to describe Eric in words, he's really just the type of person that whether you're his friend or a stranger on the street, when in his presence, you just feel happier, lighter, accepted, and... Just... At home. He isn't just a great partner, he's a great human.

In one particular meeting, we were discussing the idea of a Higher Power, and how our HPs don't have to be 'God'. We get to define our Higher Powers for ourselves in this program (which is amazing by the way - my HP is God and The Universe together).

Eric opened his comment with, "My Higher Power is a starfish." We all chuckled in gratitude for the way he made such a heavy topic seem lighter.

He went on to explain that he had an aquarium at his screen printing shop that is filled with starfish that you can't really see. Sometimes he'd see an arm sticking out here and there, waving at him, but for the most part these starfish are sort of camouflaged and always sitting invisibly behind coral or plants.

Eric went on to say that he thinks of his Higher Power in that way; though you can't always see it, you know it's there.

How sweet is that? I have always been in such awe of Eric, even before we became a couple. He has a captivating way with words and a brilliant mind.

We didn't start becoming close on a personal level until spring of 2020, at the end of April, right smack in the middle of the pandemic and a nation-wide lockdown.

We had a true and immediate connection. It was pretty clear from the get go that we were very much made for each other despite some pretty giant differences in our lifestyles. We joke about these differences often. I talk a lot (like, a lot), and he doesn't. He's the epitome of calm, and I have no chill.

Our first official date was in early May, the day before Mother's Day. Mind you, we were under a stay at home order, under quarantine. So, I couldn't exactly get a sitter for the boys, and we were still a little bit leery of even being around anyone else because - germs.

Eric very sweetly invited the boys to come along with me on our first date, knowing it was really our only option to see each other in person. This was a glowing green flag for me!

I was already wondering how my own fragile heart would handle a new relationship, and I surely wasn't making any concessions about my needs, including my children being the epicenter of my life.

We met up at Eric's print shop where he surprised us with a print he drew of our beloved sphynx cat, Naked Eli. We spent the evening chatting and laughing, screen printing shirts together and sharing pizza, cookies, and chocolate covered strawberries. The boys liked him right away, just like I did.

Chris was still alive when Eric and I first started dating and though he was no longer living with me and our divorce process was well underway, I still struggled to detach from him completely because I was so worried about him. Eric supported my efforts to continue to try to help Chris.

I also carried a lot of insecurities into our new relationship, but I was open about them and he accepted me just the same.

When I found out Chris died, Eric was the first person I called. He dropped everything he was doing to come to the house to be with me.

I cried all day long that day. All. Day. Long. And I couldn't even summon enough strength, or courage, or whatever it is that a mom needs in order to tell her children that their dad just died.

Let me try to put this all into perspective for you. Eric and I started dating in May and Chris died on July 2nd. This saint of a human ran to our sides while we grieved heavily, and supported me as I did all the things a wife does to bury her husband. Even though I was no longer Chris's wife.

Eric sat with me when I told the boys about their dad's passing. And he held my hand every step of the way, encouraging me as I began planning the visitation and funeral, writing the obituary, creating picture boards, comforting one son who was angry and distraught and the other son who was knocked down completely with sadness.

Why? Well, I think this answer is twofold. First, besides Eric being a fantastically wonderful and unselfish human being with a giant heart, he is also in Al-Anoner. This means that he, too, had experienced alcoholism on a deep and personal level himself. And, he too knows this disease well.

He had been married to a woman with alcoholism in his late twenties and early thirties. He then dated another woman with alcoholism after that until a few years before we met. It's safe to say he just understood the dire implications of a life lived with a person with alcoholism.

Second, he and the kids and I had become very close in the short time we spent as a couple before Chris lost his life. There was a lot of love already blooming within our hearts for each other.

What we later realized was that this tragedy, though extremely traumatic for us and very uncomfortable for him, brought us closer than we could have ever imagined. We made it through together, communicating with each other each step of the way and giving a lot of grace and understanding to each other.

He blew my 'will anyone ever be able to love all of me?' and 'will anyone ever be able to love my kids as their own' worries right out of the water.

Okay, it's time for another squirrel moment. I need to take a short pause and wash the mud off a few things to make them clear.

Working an Al-Anon program is hard work. It requires going back through some painful shit that would be easier to just try and forget. Just showing up to meetings once a week and expecting to magically be, poof, all better is a setup for failure. We call it 'working a program' for a reason; it takes work.

Eric most definitely slowed my fall, as he stood by my side (and my boys' sides) in Chris's final months of life, and then reached for my hand to help me stand back up once he died. It's undeniable that it would have been a hundred times harder to get through this without him.

However, without working on myself and him working on himself, we could never work. Because of how much we work on ourselves, we are able to love and understand each other in all our glory.

44

SOFT TRUTH

YOUR DECISIONS ARE NOBODY'S BUSINESS.

S pouses and family members of alcoholics deserve more credit for the things we've endured and the decisions that were mandatory for us to make.

Imma just throw this one right out there for everyone... A person who hasn't gone through what you've gone through can't understand. They just can't. This is why you don't owe anyone else an explanation of your truths or what has led you to them.

If any one part of my story really sticks with my readers, I hope it will be this one. Pay attention, beloveds, because living a joyful and peaceful life is the gift you'll be given at the end of all of this trauma.

Healing is right in front of you. You can reach out and grab it whenever you're ready; it just demands a little bit of work and reflection first. And, you're already well on your way. You'd not still be reading this book if you weren't.

Healing work is much different than the effort survival insists upon. Friend, if you can forgive yourself for all the things that you're feeling guilty about, and forgive others for everything they've done while battling their own demons, you can do anything in this world that your beautiful heart desires.

Though it can feel like a really difficult thing to process at first, forgiveness is not for anyone else but you. It's the gift of freedom that you give to yourself; your permission to move on and be happy.

What do I mean by move on? For me, it was deciding to not give up. It was letting go of all of my fears and including a new person into our family. It was moving forward from trauma. It was writing this memoir.

For you? Whatever it is that you want to move on to. Forgiveness is the key that unlocks the chains that have been holding you back and keeping you stuck.

Did I kill my husband? Absolutely not. I'll continue to pray for those individuals that have tried to place blame upon me, as well as praying for my own empathy toward them.

A dear friend, my Al-Anon sponsor, taught me this short prayer to help me through my difficult moments with difficult people: Bless them, change me. I repeat this tiny but mighty prayer to myself multiple times a day. And not just when dealing with a difficult loved one.

That cranky kid at the Taco Bell drive thru? He gets prayed for too. Bless him, change me. You wanna know why? Because we don't know his story that's why. What if he's going through some really tough stuff and is struggling to just stand on his own two feet? How could he not forget to take sour cream off this taco but add extra on that other one.

I gotta say... The unhealed parts of me like to try to sneak in and place blame and shame upon my own self too. Because though I did not kill Chris... I feel like I did fail him. And I can't stop replaying all the 'what if' scenarios in my head.

For that, I am eternally filled with pain and sorrow. That is my weight to carry, and I carry it proudly. Ultimately it's what keeps pushing me forward, sometimes even shoving me in the direction of healing and giving my children their own shot at a healthy life.

It's in this part of my journey where I'm realizing that though I may never stop grieving the loss of Chris, or even fully heal from the aftermath of such an intrusive family disease, there is still so much joy and love to be had in this rollercoaster life.

45

SOFT TRUTH

LIFE DOESN'T HAVE TO BE SO HARD.

It wasn't too long before I sat and typed these very words that I prepared myself to be a single mom for the rest of my days. I planned to rock it too. Being a mom and teacher are two things I've always been good at.

If you would have asked me a year ago how I felt about falling in love again or even the possibility of finding a lifelong partner, I would have snorted my coffee directly up my nose while laughing about the thought of it.

After you've been through so much, it can really start to feel impossible to see yourself living a happy and serene life with a healthy partner. How many freaking times do I want to put myself through more drama, ya feel me?

Besides that, it's completely terrifying to open your heart back up to someone new... You know, someone else that could very well disappoint us further and break more pieces of our stitched up hearts? Pass.

I mean look at all my baggage! It's jam packed full of grief and chaos, like can someone come sit on this for me please so I can just zip it up and keep it all inside. I often joke around and call my baggage and grief 'my griefcase'. I heard that term once and fell head over heels for it.

Plus, even *if* some angel of a man came into my life and could handle everything I bring to the table, would he want to put the effort in that it would take to raise my grieving and traumatized kids with me? Could he love them like his own? It was soooo much to think about, so I just wrote it off and washed my hands of it completely.

Can I be super blunt and honest with you about something? Remember that hard truth at the beginning of this book called: You. Fucking. Matter.? Well, guess what... When I was having these doubts about my future hopes and dreams, I clearly hadn't learned that one yet. The new me knows better.

46

SOFT TRUTH

IT'S IMPORTANT TO BELIEVE IN
SOMETHING.

I have always, for my whole entire life, wanted a partner. Ever since I can remember, I have spent many moments daydreaming about a little girl on the moon, wandering around, holding a heart shaped balloon. All the way 238,900 miles away, on Earth there was a boy on the ground, sitting under a tree, fantasizing about a girl on the moon. He'd release a heart shaped balloon into the sky for her, telling her to hold on just a little bit longer.

I had to believe that I deserved that. And, with Eric, I believe I've finally found my boy under the tree. I have no doubt that he and I have always been destined to be together, we just had a lot to learn before we could find our way to each other.

I deserve to be loved again. I deserve someone who sees my worth and cherishes me on all of my days - the beautiful ones and the ugly ones. And so do you, sweet friend. I'm certain of it. Here's something that will blow your mind: My partner also deserves all the amazing attributes I bring to the table. See, I told you I found my self worth.

Could I raise my sons to be happy, productive members of society all by myself? Undeniably. But, the right guy showed up and my kids deserve a strong and healthy man in their lives to idolize and be loved by. They deserve the patience and understanding Eric gives them as they, themselves, begin to heal from the chaos their dads have brought to their lives.

Dear friend who is still holding this book searching for hope that your own dreams will come true... I know that you may not be in the same situation as I am. Maybe you're still married and/or planning to stay married to your partner. Or, maybe you're just not ready to open your heart in a new way yet.

That's more than okay. I just want you to know that anything you want in this life is possible and available for you. Please don't give up on your hopes and dreams.

All you have to do is start to focus on yourself and your own healing, little by little, instead of spending all of your energy scrambling to fix everything and everyone else. Does that sound like a daunting task? It can be, but it doesn't have to be.

47

LEARNING TO LIVE RADICALLY

Wait it all boils down to, for me, is that I was struggling to live radically. Instead of being true to myself and to my own wants and needs, I spent entirely too much time caring about what other people thought about me or what other people thought was best for me.

I have always allowed others to dictate my life's path... Until now. I just needed to find my strength so I could find my way.

Well, guess what? I found it and I'm comin' in hot! Not only am I living my best life, I'm helping others find their way to living theirs. Boom. Strong arm emoji. Exclamation point.

I don't know about you, but the more I try to ignore my hard truths, the louder they become. I can shove them aside for a short period of time, but after a while they start raising their voices at me like, 'Heyyyyy, Lady, we're not going anywhere so you may want to pay attention to us... Or else."

You see, none of us is broken or beyond repair. One of my dearest friends refers to someone going through hard times as being bent, not broken. We each go through times in life that are excruciating and times that are beautiful - neither ever stick around forever.

In an article I wrote for www.maculardegeneration.net titled **'You're not always fine. How are you REALLY doing?'** I explained it like this: If you're currently going through something difficult, rest assured it won't always be this way. If you're not, then enjoy it because something difficult will find its way to you again. That's life.

That doesn't mean that it's always easy for me to make decisions or changes, it simply means that I no longer have room for anger, resentment, guilt, or shame in my life. Byeeee. It's what we do with those difficult times that matters.

48

SEEING THE BEAUTY IN THE WRECKAGE

I n the moment, when something is broken and shattered all over the ground, it's almost impossible to see the beauty in what's becoming.

Imagine you are standing barefoot on the ground, literally surrounded by shattered glass. You have nowhere to go but through the broken shards, with no choice but to step on the sharp fragments, slicing yourself open along the way.

As you move through it, step by step, the future looks blurry. Friend, chin up. Wipe away your tears so you can see clearly again. You know you have to keep going in order to get through it, and you know how much it's going to hurt. But, you refuse to stay stuck and cut up forever.

Once you make it to the other side, you're tired and bleeding, but you can finally start to feel relief because you know that your wounds will begin to heal at last.

The scars will always be there as a reminder of what you've been through, but you like your scars. They're part of who you are. They're a reminder of your strength and they're reassurance that you can and will recover.

Through clearer vision you'll start to realize the possibility of what new life can be born from the difficult things you've survived. Through healing, there is learning, growing, peace, and joy.

I want you to know something I wish I knew when I was still knee deep in my grief. This uncomfortable space between 'what is' and 'what will be' is transitional. It's a difficult space to be in. But, if there's even just a small touch of hope inside our hearts, then there is potential for more.

I remember one of my closest friends asking me how I was doing on one of my harder days. To which I answered, "I'm a really good robot." She chuckled then immediately corrected me, "You're not a robot, you're a transformer."

Hear this, fellow transformers: things will likely end up better than we ever thought possible if we just allow the process to happen.

Do I want to be living with a degenerative eye disease? Absolutely not. Can I grow through it, allowing it to help me live a better life? Definitely. Do any of us want to have an active alcoholic in our lives? Absolutely not. Can we grow through it too, allowing it to help us live better lives? Definitely.

We can all make the choice to keep going, keep believing, keep healing, and keep supporting one another.

Transform!

49

FINDING YOUR LIFE'S PURPOSE

B eing radical is really about becoming who you want to become. I've recently started calling this 'finding my Dharma' after hearing the term on a Mark Groves Podcast.

In Indian religion, Dharma is defined as cosmic law, and in Buddhism, it's defined as the universal truth. For me, it's been a catalyst for acknowledging the reality of what is and fulfilling my soul's purpose.

What I've noticed is that when you live radically, when you're true to yourself, you start to see things shifting around and changing for the better.

As an understatement, it has been tough to open up like this and allow others all the way in. Anyone in the entire world now has access to my deepest, darkest secrets and my most personal moments... My friends and family, Chris's friends and family, my children, and even my students and their parents. But, writing this is more than me just sharing my story and healing.

My story has the potential to help others. This is my purpose, my Dharma. If, by some small chance, I can help give others strength to find their Dharma, or if I can help save just one person's life, then it's what I need to do.

I never would have been able to even consider starting my own healing process without the help of other radical people in my life. Shout out - you know who you are, and I love you something fierce.

I call these lifesavers my parachutes. Without these women encouraging and guiding me, I would have smacked the ground less than gracefully and I wouldn't have been able to get back up. I wouldn't even know that it was possible to heal and live a happy and peaceful life without their unwavering support and pick me ups.

I've had a *hard* life, y'all. We all have, right? You get to the point where you wonder how much more you can take. There are no rules that say we each only go through a certain number of hardships and then we graduate to peace and serenity.

Luckily for people like you and me, our greatest obstacles are also our greatest teachers. You wouldn't be here reading this if you didn't believe that in your heart of hearts.

Life may not always be as easy as we'd like, but things do have a way of working out in our favor. When we start to live radically, the universe starts to shift for us, aligning us with our life's purpose.

Hey, friend? I promise you that peace and happiness are possible for you too. It hasn't been easy to be vulnerable and tell all of my experiences and faults.

I'm airing my dirty laundry - the good, the bad, and the ugly - in hopes that at one point or another you'll think, "'If this woman can come out on the other side of this feeling happy and at peace, then I can too."

If I can do it, you can too. If you need a radical human encouraging you, I'm here. Heyyyy!

Y'all, sometimes making decisions isn't about other people. Sometimes, we detach from others with the best intentions in the world, not to keep them away - but to protect ourselves.

It's important to know that when we detach, we shouldn't do it half-assed. One of my most favorite song lyrics is by The Lumineers: "The opposite of love's indifference." Don't be indifferent about your detachments.

Half-ass detachments look a lot more like giving up than protecting yourself. Like, shouting in anger, "I'm done!" and then just ghosting or avoiding the person or situation so you don't have to deal with them anymore. I get it, things do get crazy enough and painful enough to want to do this. But, it isn't healthy. Half-assed detachments will come back to bite you in your butt.

SOFT TRUTH

IT'S MORE THAN OKAY TO FALL BACK
SOMETIMES.

L ook, just because we're healing and starting to live more peacefully doesn't mean that our insecurities and difficult memories won't creep in every once in a while. Actually, you can guarantee that it's going to happen. Annnnd usually at really inopportune times.

Do you think I wrote this book without shedding any tears? Nope. I freaking bawled my way through it... Like ugly crying you guys. Something that has really helped me understand these intense bouts of grief is the idea that if something is hysterical, it's historical. In other words, sometimes memories and emotions pop up from your past and cause big, huge feelings. It's a thing that's going to happen.

This is never ever going to stop hurting. So, when it does, I allow myself to feel it. I just no longer sit in it and let it fester.

I'm gonna let you in on a little secret... I actually kind of like these painful bursts of emotions from my past. They're reminders to me that this mattered.

It changed my life. It changed my children's lives. It took away Chris's life. And that all matters. A lot. I want the reminders; the scars and the bruises are important to me.

I'm also glad for the reminders of how far I've come and to appreciate every tiny, miniscule thing in my life. Tears and pain bring gratitude. I'm not mad at it.

My wish for you is that you, too, are able to find your glimmer of hope and gratitude for all the 'bad' in your life so you can find your way to the good at last.

It's time for your, 'Whoa, it's me!' instead of 'Oh, woe is me', dear one. You're allowed to change. And you don't need anyone else's permission or approval. This is your life and you've been spending the only one you get - suffering. Well, guess what world, we're putting our feet down. We're done with that shit.

I believe in you, sweet friends. Deep breaths. You got this. One day at a time.

I'd love to meet each and every one of you and hear your story! Please reach out to me. You can find me on Instagram at @ididnotkillmyhusband. If you send me a PM, I will write back as soon as I can. I'm looking forward to getting to know you better.

If you're looking for an Al-Anon meeting for yourself, go to www.Al-anon.org and click 'how to find a meeting'.

ABOUT THE AUTHOR

Annie, her partner, Eric, and her two young sons live in the small town she has taught elementary school in for seventeen years.

Through her turbulent life experiences, Annie has found a deep passion for educating people from ages 8 to 98. Whether teaching children in her classroom, inspiring her peers through her memoir and social media pages, or writing informational articles for the elderly through the website she writes for, Annie finds purpose through helping others navigate their own personal struggles in life.

Along her life-long journey, battling her way to happiness and peace for herself and her family, Annie has gained a vast array of experiential expertise on complex issues. These issues include: Emotional abuse, infidelity, divorce, suicidal ideation, grief, anxiety, depression, narcissism, the family disease of alcoholism, Al-Anon Twelve Step Programs, Alcoholics Anonymous Programs, mental health therapy, and macular degeneration (and blindness).

At the age of 26, Annie was diagnosed with myopic macular degeneration after noticing a small blind spot in her right eye. In an attempt to understand and accept her diagnosis as well as tame her worries about her future, she sought support and knowledge in online communities. She now writes patient advocate articles which are published to Health Union's macular degeneration website and social media page.

Though she keeps busy teaching full time, writing articles and moderating HU's website, writing memoirs and children's books, and managing her professional Instagram author page, Annie prioritizes herself and her family.

Annie and her family's emotional healing from the devastation they each encountered from living with active alcoholics, is of utmost importance to her. Her family focuses a lot of their time and energy working on recovery. All four members of their little Ohana attend mental health therapy sessions with therapists. She and Eric attend Al-Anon meetings together, and both are 'working the twelve steps' of the program with their insightful sponsors.

Annie's passion for helping others centers on the ideology of living a holistic, healthy lifestyle, and ending the stigma surrounding mental health therapy.

In her down time, you can find Annie writing, cooking, jogging or taking long walks - always seeking the beauty and symbolism of colorful sunrises and sunsets. The quiet and stillness of the country roads that surround her home helps her to recharge and focus on what's important.

Annie also enjoys going to concerts with her friends and watching her sons play soccer, basketball, guitar, and drums. Her privations in life have afforded her the opportunity to see the importance of living her best life. This memoir is Annie's paper pride and joy. She's elated to share her experience, strength, and hope with the world. You can contact Annie through Instagram @ididnotkillmyhusband.

ACKNOWLEDGMENTS

First, to my two sons: You both have been through so much and yet you amaze me every day with your continued ability to smile and find the light. You've risen above everything life has thrown at you and though I wish I could take away all of your pain, I know that you are stronger because of it. I have no doubt you will both do big things in this world. My hope for both of you is that you never forget how strong and resilient you are, how loved you are, how brave you are, and how capable you are. All that has happened to you does not define you, but teaches you. Remember that the universe is always conspiring for us even though it doesn't always feel that way. Everything that happens has purpose even though we may not always get to know why right away. I am so proud of the way you both refuse to allow your hardships in life to take away your big hearts. You're the strongest young men I know. I love you both something fierce.

Thank you for saving my life and giving me the chance to do better at being your mom. It's been an honor and privilege every step of the way. Keep on shining, my loves.

To Eric, my saving grace, and the love of my life: Thank you for being my biggest fan and loudest cheerleader, my bedside editor, and confidante. Without your consistent encouragement, I would have given up a thousand times. I don't know how I'm lucky enough to be the one who gets to walk by your side for the rest of this crazy life, but I want to thank you for seeing past our 'griefcase' and loving us anyway. From the moment we met outside of 'the rooms of Al-Anon', you've put a smile on my face, held my hand, helped me pick up my broken pieces, nourished my soul, loved my children as your own, and nudged me forward when I lost my 'brave'. I know that Chris is eternally thankful for how well you care for our little Ohana. I've waited my whole entire life for you. And I am eternally thankful for every single difficult thing that's happened to both of us because it all conspired beautifully to bring us together. What a plot twist you were. I love you from the moon to the trees.

To my late husband, Chris: I promised your soul that I'd never stop telling our story, aspiring to help as many people as possible. Your death was not in vain. I'm sorry for how much you suffered through this life here on earth and I'm sorry that it took me so long to understand all of this. This is how we will move forward together, saving lives and giving hope. I see so much of you in the boys, your light still shines so brightly. They got all the best parts of you and I'm grateful for that gift every day. I find comfort in knowing that you are no longer in pain. Keep watching over the boys from above and Eric and I will take care of the rest down here. I see your signs from the other side and I thank you for your encouragement to keep going. You are greatly missed by everyone who ever had the privilege of knowing you. Rest peacefully, my dear friend.

To Casey, in true Annie and Casey fashion, we took this hard thing and made it softer. Thank you for the zillion texts, edits, and words of encouragement. I could not have done this without you by my side. It's always been me and you. I can't wait to see what the rest of our friendship has in store.

Annie

REFERENCES

National Institute on Alcohol Abuse and Alcoholism, https://www.niaaa.nih.gov/.

Al-Anon Family Groups. *How Al-Anon Works.* Al-Anon Family Groups.

americanaddictioncenters.org. "Alcohol Withdrawal Symptoms, Treatment, and Timeline." https://americanaddictioncenters. org/withdrawal-timelines-treatments/alcohol.

Benton, Sarah A. "Being Sober Vs Being in Recovery." *Psychology Today,* 2010. *www.psychologytoday.com,* https:// www.psychologytoday.com/us/blog/the-high-functioning-alcoholic/201005/being-sober-versus-being-in-recovery. Accessed 17 March 2020.

Made in the USA
Monee, IL
13 May 2021